Kweller Prep

SAT Hard Math Workbook

Douglas S. Kovel

Copyright © 2017 Douglas S. Kovel

All rights reserved.

No part of this work may be reproduced, stored in a retrieval system, or transmitted in any form or by any means, including electronic, mechanical, photocopy, or recording, without the written permission of the author. For more information, please email info@kwellerprep.com.

ISBN-13:978-1979434591

Contents

Week 1: Linear Equations and Systems of Linear Equations 4
Week 2: Linear Functions and Linear Equations in Context 14
Week 3: Systems of Linear Equations in Context and Systems of Linear Inequalities 24
Week 4: Rates and Measurements 32
Week 5: Percents, Linear and Exponential Growth, and Graphs 37
Week 6: Data I 42
Week 7: Data II 50
Week 8: Advanced Algebraic Operations 59
Week 9: Advanced Algebraic Operations II 65
Week 10: Advanced Algebraic Equations 73
Week 11: Advanced Quadratics and Polynomials 82
Week 12: Exponential Functions in Context and Manipulating Expressions 90
Week 13: Polygons 97
Week 14: Circles, Solid Geometry, Trigonometry, and Complex Numbers 102
Key 125
Week 1 126
Week 2 129
Week 3 132
Week 4 132
Week 5 137
Week 6 139
Week 7 141
Week 8 142
Week 9 145
Week 10 147
Week 11 150
Week 12 152
Week 13 154
Week 14 159
About the Author 163
Appendix 164

Week 1: Linear Equations and Systems of Linear Equations

No Calculator

1. Which expression equals 0 for some value of x?
   A. $|x+2|+2$
   B. $|x-2|-2$ ⟵ circled
   C. $|2-x|+2$
   D. $|x-2|+2$

$$2.4(h+2) = .3h + 7.95$$

2. What is the value of h in the equation above?

   $2.4h + 4.8 = 0.3h + 7.95$
   $(2.1)h = 3.15$
   $\boxed{h = 1.5}$

$$kx + 4 = k(x+4) + 1.2$$

3. If $x = -2$, what is the value of k in the equation above?

   $-2k + 4 = -2k + 4k + 1.2$
   $-2k + 4 = 2k + 1.2$
   $4 - 1.2 = 4k$
   $2.8 = 4k \longrightarrow \boxed{0.7 = k}$

$$y = \frac{7(5t - 4c)}{2} - 30$$

4. In the equation above, t equals 50 and y equals 705. What is the value of c?

   $y = \frac{35t - 28c}{2} - 30$
   $\frac{(2(y+30)) - 35t}{-28} = \boxed{c = 10}$

5. Line k has the coordinates (1,7) and (6, 17). Line m is parallel to line k and contains the coordinates (1,5) and (4, n). What is the value of n?

   $\frac{\Delta y}{\Delta x}$ $\frac{17-7}{6-1} = \frac{10}{5} = 2$

   $\frac{5-n}{1-4} = 2$ $\frac{5-n}{-3} = 2$
   $5 - n = -6$
   $\boxed{11 = n}$

Week 1   4

6. A line has a slope of $\frac{1}{9}$ and runs through the origin. Which of the following is a point on that line?
   A. (-9,1)
   B. (3,27)
   C. (1,9)
   D. (27,3) ✓

$$\frac{5(x-3)}{2} = \frac{10(x-5)}{3}$$

7. What is the value of x in the equation above?

   $15(x-3) = 20(x-10)$
   $15x - 45 = 20x - 200$
   $-45 = 5x - 200$
   $155 = 5x$
   $31 = x$

8. Two different points are 5 units away from the coordinate $x = -2$. Which of the following equations models all possible values of x?
   A. $|x - 5| = 2$
   B. $|x + 5| = 2$ ✓
   C. $|x - 2| = 5$
   D. $|x + 2| = 5$

9. A line graphed in the xy-plane has a positive slope and negative y-intercept. Which of the following cannot be a point on the line?
   A. (2,5)
   B. (-2,5) ✓
   C. (-2,-5)
   D. (2,-5)

Week 1

$$ax - 6ay = 1$$

10. In the equation above, a is a nonzero constant. The graph of the equation in the xy-plane is a line. What is the slope of the line?

    A. $\frac{1}{6}$
    B. $\frac{1}{6a}$
    C. $6a$
    D. 6

11. In the xy-plane a line contains the points $(-n, k)$ and $(-k, n)$ when $k + n = 0$ and k and $n \neq 0$. What is the slope of the line?

12. Line k contains the points $(8,3)$ and $(10,4)$. If line m is perpendicular to line k and contains the point $(1, c)$ and $(5,10)$, what is the value of c?

13. In the xy-plane, what is the x-intercept of the line with the equation $6x + 7y = 15$?

Week 1

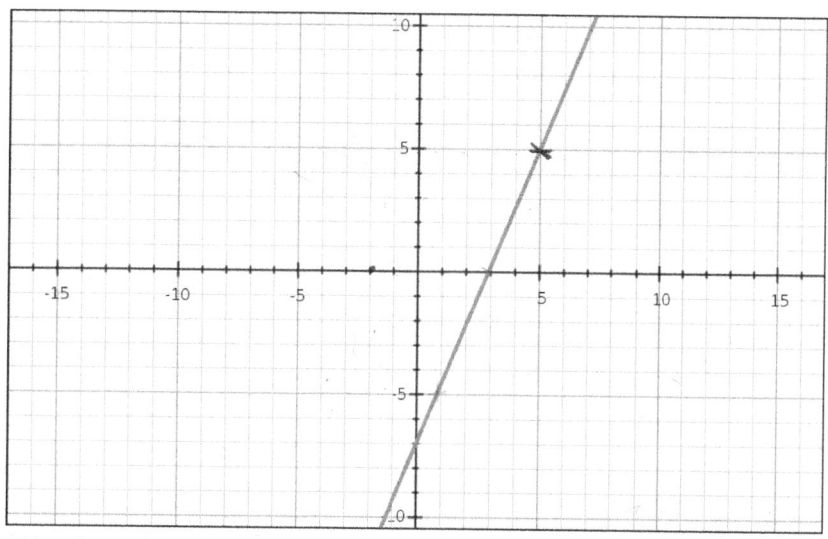

14. The line above contains the points (0,-7) and (5,5,). Which of the following is the y-intercept of the line that is parallel to the line above and contains the point (-2,0)?

(0, 5)

$$\frac{x}{y} = 8$$
$$2(y + 3) = x - 6$$

15. In the system of equations above, what is the value of y?
    A. 2 ✓
    B. 6
    C. 8
    D. 16

$x = 8y$
$x = 2y + 12$
$8y = 2y + 12$ $6y = 12$
                   $y = 2$

$$\frac{5}{2}a + 4 = \frac{1}{2}(5a + 4)$$

16. What is the solution to the equation above?
    A. The solution is $a = \frac{5}{4}$
    B. The solution is $a = 5$
    C. There are no solutions ✓
    D. There are an infinite number of solutions

$\frac{5}{2}a + 2 = \frac{5}{2}a + 4$
$2 \neq 4$

Week 1

17. What is the value of x in the equation above?

$$.08(250 - x) = .72$$

$$250 - \left(\frac{0.72}{0.08}\right) = x = 241$$

18. One solution to the equation above is $x = 3$. What is the other solution?

$$4|-2x + 8| + 2 = 10$$

$$4|-2x+8| = 8$$
$$|-2x+8| = 2$$
$$x = 5$$

Calculator

19. The line with the equation $\frac{5}{3}x + 2y = 1$ is graphed on the coordinate plane. What is the x-coordinate of the x-intercept?

$$\frac{5}{3}x + 0 = 1$$
$$x = \frac{3}{5}$$

20. If $2(x + y) = 5$, what is the value of $x + y$?

A. $\frac{2}{5}$
B. $\frac{5}{2}$ ⊙
C. 3
D. 7

$$x+y = \frac{5}{2}$$

21. If $2a + 4b = 12$, what is the value of $\frac{1}{3}a + \frac{2}{3}b$?

$$\frac{a+2b}{3} = \frac{6}{3}$$
$$\frac{a}{3} + \frac{2b}{3} = 2$$

$$2 = \frac{1}{3}a + \frac{2}{3}b$$

Week 1

22. If $\frac{1}{2}(3x + 8y) = 20$, what is the value of $15x + 40y - 10$?

$15x + 4y = 20$ (student work)
$15x + 40 = 200$

$\boxed{190}$

23. If a line includes the points $(0,0)$, $(4, k)$ and $(k, 3)$, what is a possible value of k?

A. $\sqrt{\frac{4}{3}}$

B. $\frac{4}{3}$

C. $\sqrt{12}$ ✓

D. 12

$\frac{k}{4} = \frac{3}{k}$

$k^2 = 12$

$$\frac{3}{2}x + \frac{1}{3}y = 4$$
$$x + 4y = -20$$

24. In the system of equations shown above, what is the value of $x - y$?

25. If $20a + 20b = 48$, what is the value of $5a + 5b + 2$?

Week 1

9

$$\frac{1}{2}x + \frac{1}{4}y = 2$$
$$\frac{1}{8}x + \frac{1}{8}y = 8$$

26. What is the solution to the system of equations above?
    A. (104, -200)
    B. (-56, 120)
    C. (-54, 108)
    D. (16, 48)

$$x = \frac{1}{4}y$$
$$182 - 3y = 14x$$

27. If the lines with the equations above were graphed on the xy-plane, what would be the x-coordinate of the point of intersection?

$$ax + bx = 20$$
$$8x + 6x = 100$$

28. If the system of equations above has an infinite number of solutions, what is the value of $a - b$?

$$ax + bx = 12$$
$$4x + 7x = 36$$

29. If the system of equations above has an infinite number of solutions, what is the value of $\frac{a}{b}$?

$$ax + 4y = 89$$
$$6x + 20y = 8$$
30. If the system of equations above has no solution, what is the value of a?

$$ax + 7y = 13$$
$$3x + 5y = 10$$
31. If the system of equations above has no solution, what is the value of a?

$$2x + 3y = 13$$
$$ax + 8y = 10$$
32. If the system of equations above has no solution, what is the value of a?

$$a = 2b + 4c$$
$$d = 3b + 5c$$
33. If d is 1 more than a, which equation shows the relationship between b and c?
   A. $b = c + 1$
   B. $b = -c + 1$
   C. $b = c - 1$
   D. $b = -c - 1$

$$3x - 1 = 4y + 2z$$
$$3x = 8y - 4z$$

34. Which of the following shows the relationship between y and z in the equations above?

    A. $z = 4y - 6$
    B. $z = \frac{3}{2}y + \frac{1}{6}$
    C. $z = \frac{2}{3}y - \frac{1}{6}$
    D. $z = \frac{3}{2}y + \frac{1}{3}$

35. What is the slope of the line that is perpendicular to the line $y = 5$?

    A. $\frac{-1}{5}$
    B. 0
    C. 5
    D. Undefined

36. In the xy-plane, a line has a slope of 3 and intercepts $(p, 0)$ and $(0, n)$. If n is 8 more than p, what is the value of $n + p$?

Week 1

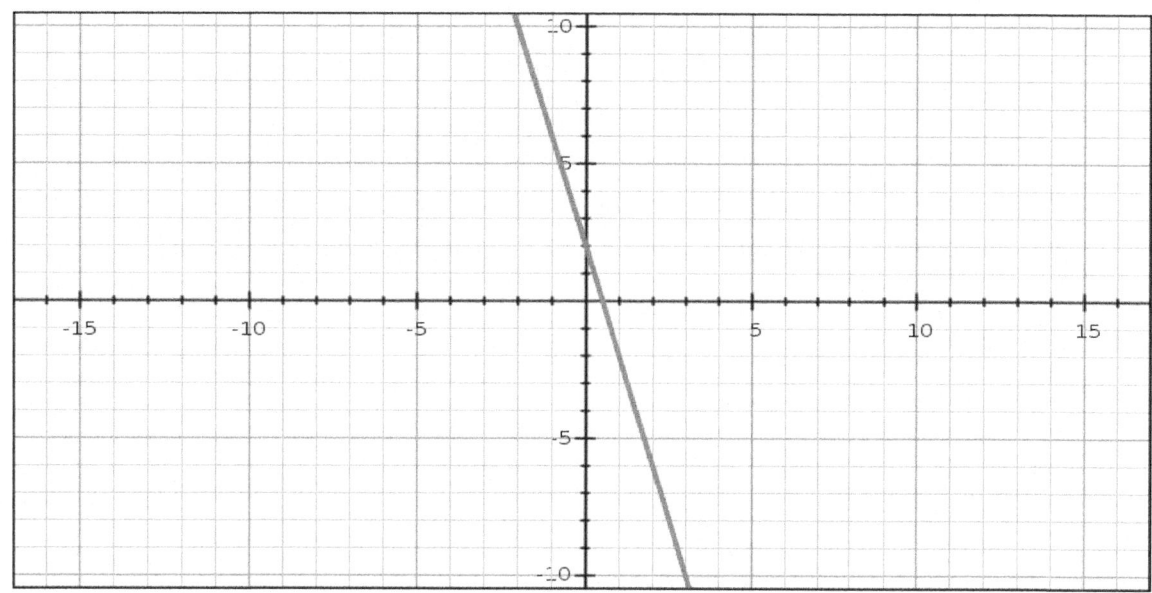

37. The graph of linear function f is shown in the xy-plane above. The linear function g is perpendicular to f and passes through the point (4,5). What is $g(0)$?

38. On the xy-coordinate plane, segments AB and BC are perpendicular. The coordinates of A are (0,0), the coordinates of B are (2,3), and the coordinates of C are $(p, 0)$, where p is a constant. What is the value of p?
   A. 5.5
   B. 6
   C. 6.25
   D. 6.5

Week 1

Week 2: Linear Functions and Linear Equations in Context

No Calculator

1. Dan increases the number of miles he walks each week by a constant amount. If he walks 10 miles in week 4 and 16 miles in week 8, by how many miles does he increase his walk each week?
   A. 1.5
   B. 1
   C. .75
   D. .5

$$n = -3T + 20$$

2. The formula above relates the number of customers for hot coffee at a concession stand, n, to the temperature in degrees Celsius. Which of the following is true?
   A. As the temperature increases by 1 degree, the number of customers increases by 3
   B. As the temperature decreases by 1 degree, the number of customers increases by 3
   C. As the number of customers increases by 1, the temperature decreases by 3 degrees
   D. As the number of customers decreases by 1, the temperature increases by 3 degrees

$$y = \frac{x+5}{2}$$

3. In the equation above, as x increases by 1, y increases by how much?

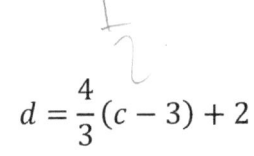

$$d = \frac{4}{3}(c - 3) + 2$$

4. Which of the following statements are true about the equation above?
   I. As c increases by 1, d increases by $\frac{4}{3}$.
   II. As c increases by 1, d increases by .75
   III. As d increases by 1, c increases by $\frac{4}{3}$.
   IV. As d increases by 1, c increases by .75

   A. I only
   B. II only
   C. II and III
   D. I and IV

5. The height of an ancient structure is modeled by the equation $h = -\frac{1}{400}t + 482$ where h is the height in feet and t is the number of years since it has been built. According to the function, which of the following is true?
   A. The height decreases by 400 feet each year
   B. The height decreases by $\frac{1}{4}$ foot every 100 years
   C. The height decreases by 400 feet every 100 years
   D. The height decreases by 1 foot every 4,000 years

6. The population of a town, in <u>thousands</u>, is modeled by the function $f(t) = 300 - 50t$, such that t is the number of years that have passed since 1980. Which of the following is true about the change in population since 1980?
   A. Every 5 years, the population increases by 300,000.
   B. Every year, the population decreases by 50.
   C. Every year, the population decreases by 50,000.
   D. Every year, the population increases by 50,000.

7. Identical pails are stacked one on top of the other. If n represents the number of pails, h represents the height of the pails in inches, and $n > 1$, by how many inches does the height of the stack increase for each additional pail, when $h = 2n + 8$?
   A. 1
   B. 2
   C. 4
   D. 8

8. $A = 2p + 40$ models the relationship between the area of a fence, in square feet, and the perimeter of the fence, in feet. As the area increases by 1 square foot, by how many feet does the perimeter increase?

9. The equation $y = 33 - .95x$ models the height of a certain candle after it starts burning. In the equation, y is the height of the candle, in centimeters, and x is the amount of time for which it has been burning, in hours. What is the meaning of the y-intercept in this equation?
   A. The number of hours for which the candle burns
   B. The number of inches by which the height of the candle decreases each hour
   C. The age of the candle at the time it is burned
   D. The height of the candle, in centimeters, at the time it is burned

Week 2

10. A farmer has c cows and h horses on his farm. If he has three times as many cows as horses, which of the following must be true?
    A. $3c = h$
    B. $3h = c$
    C. $c + h = 3$
    D. $c = h + 3$

11. On a certain planet, as depth from sea level decreases by 20 feet, the temperature decreases by 1 degree. At sea level, the temperature is 30 degrees Celsius. Which equations shows the relationship between temperature, C, and depth, f?
    A. $C = 30 - \frac{f}{20}$
    B. $C = 30 - 20f$
    C. $C = 20 - 30f$
    D. $C = \frac{f}{20}$

12. As of 2016, the tallest steel roller coaster in the United States is about 36 feet taller than that of the second highest. If the sum of their heights is 876 feet, what is the approximate height of the tallest roller coaster, in feet?
    A. 400
    B. 420
    C. 456
    D. 492

13. Sheree studied for a combined total of 1 hour and 27 minutes on Tuesday and Wednesday. She studied for twice as much time on Wednesday as on Tuesday. For how many minutes did she study on Wednesday?

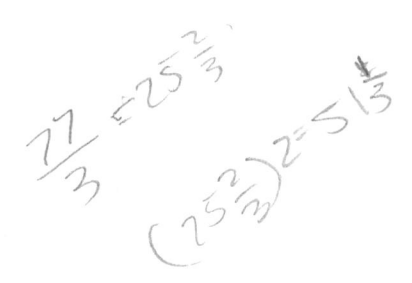

Week 2

x	1	2	3	4
y	$\frac{7}{3}$	$\frac{11}{3}$	5	$\frac{19}{3}$

14. For the table above, which of the following equations relates y to x?

    A. $y = x + \frac{7}{3}$

    B. $y = \frac{4}{3}x + 1$

    C. $y = 1(\frac{4}{3})^x$

    D. $y = \frac{49}{33}(\frac{11}{7})^x$

15. There are twice as many birds as lizards in a certain pet store. Which equation models this situation when there are b birds and l lizards?

    A. $b + 2 = l$

    B. $l + 2 = b$

    C. $2b = l$

    D. $2l = b$

16. The average number of customers per day for hot chocolate decreases by 900 for every 10 degrees the temperature rises above 0 degrees Celsius. If the average number of customers when the temperature is 0 degrees is 562, which of the following functions shows the relationship between the average number of customers, $f(t)$, and temperature in degrees Celsius, t?

    A. $f(t) = 562 - 900t$

    B. $f(t) = 90 - 562t$

    C. $f(t) = 900 - 562t$

    D. $f(t) = 562 - 90t$

17. The temperature of liquid going through a heating system increases at a constant rate from 24 degrees Celsius to 100 degrees Celsius in 19 seconds. Which of the following functions represents the temperature in Celsius, T, after s seconds, where $0 \leq s \leq 19$?

    A. $T = 24 + 2s$

    B. $T = 24 + 4s$

    C. $T = 24 + 8s$

    D. $T = 24 + 19s$

Week 2

18. To order books in bulk, a company is charged $10 per book for the first 400 books. After the first 400 books are ordered, the price drops to $8 a book. Which function models the cost, C, in dollars, of buying x books, when $x > 400$?
    A. $C = 10x + 8$
    B. $C = 10(x - 400) + 8x$
    C. $C = 4{,}000 + 8x$
    D. $C = 4{,}000 + 8(x - 400)$

19. The boiling point of water at sea level is about 100 degrees Celsius. For every 100 feet above sea level, the boiling point drops about .1 degrees. Which of the following models best approximates the relationship between boiling point, B, in Celsius, and height above sea level, h, in feet?
    A. $B = 100 - .1t$
    B. $B = 100 - .001t$
    C. $B = -.001t$
    D. $B = 100 - .1(100)t$

20. Between 1992 and 2003, the budget of a certain state government department decreased from $2.8 billion to $1.1 billion. Which of the following models the budget, $f(t)$, in billions of dollars, t years after 1992?
    A. $f(t) = 2.8 - \frac{17}{110}t$
    B. $f(t) = 2.8 + \frac{17}{110}t$
    C. $f(t) = 2.8 - \frac{39}{110}t$
    D. $f(t) = 2.8 + \frac{39}{110}t$

21. On a certain planet, the temperature is -5 degrees Celsius 50 kilometers above ground and -25 degrees Celsius 75 kilometers above ground. For every 10 kilometers above the ground, the temperature decreases by n degrees Celsius. What is the value of n?

Week 2

Calculator

22. A magazine has 1,800 subscribers in its opening month. Each month thereafter during the first 4 months, the magazine gains an average of 2,000 new subscribers and loses an average of 500 subscribers. Which of the following equations best relates subscribers, s, to months, m, to the magazine, m months after its opening month for $0 \leq m \leq 4$?
    A. $s = 1800 - 500m$
    B. $s = 1800 + 2000m$
    C. $s = 1800 + .75m$
    D. $s = 1800 + 1500m$

23. Catalina creates figurines that she sells at a fair. Each figure costs her $8 in materials to make, and she sells each figure for $25. Which of the following equations models her profit, P, in dollars, for selling x figurines?
    A. $P = 17x$
    B. $P = 25x$
    C. $P = 25x - 11$
    D. $P = 33x$

Questions 24 to 26 are based on the situation below.

$$d = 565 - 120t$$

The distance of a train from a train station in Town A to Town B in miles, d, t hours after it departs is modeled by the equation above.

24. What is the meaning of 565 in the equation above?
    A. The speed of the train in miles per hour
    B. The distance the train needs to travel to reach Town B, in miles
    C. The number of hours it takes to travel from Town A to Town B
    D. The time, in minutes, it takes the train to travel from Town A to Town B

25. What is the meaning of 120 in the equation above?
    A. The speed of the train in miles per hour
    B. The distance the train needs to travel to reach Town B, in miles
    C. The number of hours it takes to travel from Town A to Town B
    D. The time, in minutes, it takes the train to travel from Town A to Town B

26. How many hours will it take the train to travel between the two cities? (Round to the nearest tenth.)

Week 2

Questions 27 and 28 are based on the table below.

Time (days)	Plant height (cm)
0	1.41
7	2.16
14	2.67
21	3.19
28	4.02
35	4.73

27. The function $f(x) = ax + b$ represents the height after x days during a particular time period. What does a mean?
    A. The predicted height at the start of the period
    B. The predicted increase in height each day of the period
    C. The predicted height at the end of the period
    D. The total number of centimeters grown during the period

28. On the interval day 7 to day 14, which of the following models best approximates the height after t days of growth?
    A. $h = .51t + 2.16$
    B. $h = .072t + 1.66$
    C. $h = 13.7t - 93.74$
    D. $h = .104t + 1.43$

Units Sold	Revenue (in dollars)
6000	5,900,000
8,100	8,000,000
9,500	9,400,000
11,200	11,100,000

29. For the table above, which of the following linear functions relates revenue, R, to units sold, x, when $6000 \leq x \leq 11200$?
    A. $R = .001x + 100$
    B. $R = 5.2x + 27.8$
    C. $R = 1000x - 100,000$
    D. $R = 1700x + 900,000$

Week 2

20

Mortgage (in dollars)	Price (in dollars)
1,000	120,000
1,510	180,000
1,935	230,000
2,955	350,000
4,570	540,000

30. For the table above, which of the following shows the linear relationship between price in thousands of dollars and mortgage (in dollars)?
    A. $m(p) = 8.5p - 20$
    B. $m(p) = 6.5p + 340$
    C. $m(p) = 3p - 260$
    D. $m(p) = 7.5p + 100$

31. Each umbrella is $20 more than each hat. If two hats and three umbrellas cost $385, how much does one umbrella cost?

32. For five consecutive even integers, the sum of the first and the third integers is 16 more than the fifth integer. What is the second integer?

Population of Town A

Year	Population
2005	905
2010	950

33. The rate of population growth in the table above is linear. Which equation shows the relationship between population, P, and time, t, t years after 2005?
    A. $P = 905 + 45t$
    B. $P = 905 + 9t$
    C. $P = 905 - 9(t - 2005)$
    D. $P = 905 + 9(t - 2005)$

Week 2

Number of Smaller Tables	Maximum Number of People
1	10
2	16
3	22

34. At a restaurant, smaller tables can be grouped together to form larger tables. The table above shows the maximum number of people that can fit in the first three possible arrangements of tables. Which of the following expressions can be used to represent the maximum number of people that can fit at a table when n smaller tables are used?
    A. $10n$
    B. $5n + 5$
    C. $6n + 4$
    D. $8n$

Student 1: $y = 50 - .20x$

Student 2: $y = 48 - .43x$

35. The average amount of time in seconds, y, it takes two students to type a certain note x weeks after starting a typing class is shown above. Which of the following best explains the relationship between seconds needed to type the note for the two students?
    A. y increases faster for Student 1 as x increases
    B. y increases faster for Student 2 as x increases
    C. y decreases faster for Student 1 as x increases
    D. y decreases faster for Student 2 as x increases

36. A manager earns $20.00 per hour worked until 5:00 p.m. and $2.40 more per hour for each hour worked 5:00 p.m. and after. If the manager worked 50 hours last week and h hours were on or after 5:00 p.m., which function models the manager's total earnings?
    A. $f(h) = 20h + 2.40(h - 50)$
    B. $f(h) = 20(h - 50) + 2.40h$
    C. $f(h) = 20(50 - h) + 22.40h$
    D. $f(h) = 22.40(50 - h) + 20h$

37. The number of gadgets that Brita has to repair, N, can be modeled by the linear equation $N = 120 - 16t$, where t is the number of hours for which she works. What is the meaning of the x-intercept on the graph of this equation in the xy-plane?
   A. Brita can fix about 16 gadgets an hour
   B. Brita starts with 120 gadgets to fix
   C. It takes Brita about 7.5 hours of work to fix all the gadgets
   D. Brita will repair about 7.5 gadgets per hour

x	$h(x)$
-6	-15
-2	-7
3	3

38. In the table that represents the linear function above, what is the value of $h(5)$?

39. The first row of an auditorium has 20 seats. There are 40 total rows. Each row after the first has 4 more seats than the row before it. How many seats are in the last row?
   A. $20 + 4^{40}$
   B. $20 + 4(39)$
   C. $20 + 4(40)$
   D. $40(20 + 4)$

Week 3: Systems of Linear Equations in Context and Systems of Linear Inequalities

No Calculator

1. 60 teams in groups of 3 or 4 students each competed in a contest. There were 219 students in total. How many teams had 4 people?

2. At a store, bracelets sell for $40 each and necklaces sell for $60 each. One day, 80 bracelets and necklaces are sold for a total of $3,700. How many of the 80 pieces of jewelry sold were necklaces?

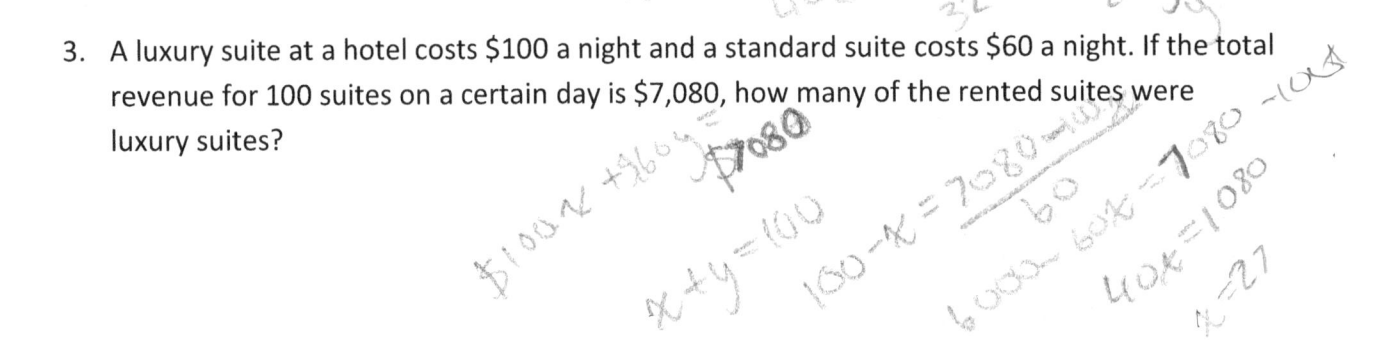

3. A luxury suite at a hotel costs $100 a night and a standard suite costs $60 a night. If the total revenue for 100 suites on a certain day is $7,080, how many of the rented suites were luxury suites?

4. It costs Farad $2 to bake a dozen bagels and he sells each dozen for $6. He also pays an $81 vendor's fee. At least how many dozens of bagels does he need to sell to recoup the vendor fee?
   A. 14
   B. 20
   C. 21
   D. 40

5. A pack of black ink cartridges sells for $30 and a pack of colored ink cartridges sell for $40. One day, a store sells 3 more packs of color cartridges than black cartridges. The total revenue for black and color cartridge packs was $820. How many packages of black ink cartridges were sold?

6. A company needs to hire a minimum of 10 new employees. Analysts will be paid $800 a week and associates will earn $1,200 a week. The company needs to hire at least 4 analysts and 2 associates. The company's weekly salary budget for the new employees is $14,500. Which system of inequalities models the possible number of x analysts and y associates that can be hired?

A. $x + y \geq 10$
$800x + 1200y \geq 14500$
$x \geq 4$
$y \geq 2$

B. $x + y \geq 10$
$800x + 1200y \leq 14500$
$x \geq 4$
$y \geq 2$

C. $x + y \leq 10$
$800x + 1200y \leq 14500$
$x \geq 4$
$y \geq 2$

D. $x + y \leq 10$
$800x + 1200y \leq 14500$
$x \leq 4$
$y \leq 2$

7. A pole is made with 16 connected rods, each measuring at least 140 centimeters and at most 150 centimeters. If x is the length of the pole in centimeters, which of the following models all possible values of x?

A. $16 \leq x \leq 150$
B. $140 \leq x \leq 150$
C. $2240 \leq x \leq 2400$
D. $2400 \leq x \leq 3640$

8. A teacher spends at least $40 to purchase utensils for a bake sale. She must purchase plates and forks. Each set of forks costs $5, and each set of plates costs $8. If the number of sets of forks is f and the number of sets of plates is p, which of the following systems of inequalities models this situation?
   A. $5f + 8p \geq 40$
      $p + f \leq 1$
   B. $5f + 8p \leq 40$
      $p + f \leq 1$
   C. $5f + 8p \geq 40$
      $p \geq 1$
      $f \geq 1$
   D. $5f + 8p \leq 40$
      $p \geq 1$
      $f \geq 1$

9. Red blocks cost $4.50 each, and white blocks cost $5.35 each. There are twice as many red blocks as white blocks, and the total cost of the blocks is at least $100. Which of the following systems of inequalities models this situation, where r is the number of red blocks and w is the number of white blocks?
   A. $4.50r + 5.35w \geq 100$
      $r = 2w$
   B. $4.50r + 5.35w \geq 100$
      $2r = w$
   C. $9r + 5.35w \geq 100$
      $r = 2w$
   D. $9r + 5.35w \geq 100$
      $2r = w$

Week 3

10. A teacher has $120 to spend on magazines costing $2.50 each and books costing $5.60 each for her students. She needs to buy both books and magazines. Which system of inequalities models this situation where m is the number of magazines and b is the number of books bought?

   A. $2.50m + 5.60p \geq 120$
   $m \geq 1$
   $b \geq 1$

   B. $2.50m + 5.60p \leq 120$
   $m + b \leq 1$

   C. $2.50m + 5.60p \leq 120$
   $m \geq 1$
   $b \geq 1$

   D. $2.50m + 5.60p \geq 120$
   $m + b \leq 1$

11. A small boat carrying cargo has a weight capacity of 2,000 pounds. A company is transporting sofas that weigh 75 pounds each and tables that weigh 35 pounds each. If the weight of the employees and all other equipment on the boat is 300 pounds, what is the maximum number sofas that can be transported if there are 30 tables on the boat?

   A. 7
   B. 8
   C. 9
   D. 10

$$y > 2x + 7$$
$$2x > 2$$

12. Which of the following gives all y coordinates that satisfy the system of inequalities above?

   A. $y > -5$
   B. $y > -4$
   C. $y > 1$
   D. $y > 9$

13. A maximum of 2,000 tickets can be sold to fill an auditorium for a play. Tickets for children cost $5 each and tickets for adults cost $8 each. A total of x children's tickets and y adult tickets are sold. In order to make a profit, the theater must sell more than $12,000 worth of tickets. Which system of inequalities models the number of tickets that can be sold for the theater to make a profit?

   A. $5x + 8y < 2,000$ and $x + y > 12,000$
   B. $x + y \geq 2,000$ and $5x + 8y > 12,000$
   C. $x + y \leq 2,000$ and $5x + 8y < 12,000$
   D. $x + y \leq 2,000$ and $5x + 8y > 12,000$

Week 3

14. It takes Ira 18 minutes to walk to the library. It takes her 6 minutes to get to the library by bus, which arrives at the bus stop every 25 minutes. The number of minutes Ira waits for the bus, x, is some value between 0 and 25 inclusive. Solving for which inequality yields all values of x for which it is faster for Ira to walk than to take the bus?
    A. $x - 6 < 18$
    B. $x - 6 > 18$
    C. $x + 6 < 18$
    D. $x + 6 > 18$

15. 10 artists present entries for acceptance into a talent showcase. Some of the artists submit 2 works each and some of them submit 3 works each. If x is the number of artists submitting 2 works, what expression gives the total number of works submitted by all 10 artists?
    A. $10x$
    B. $20x$
    C. $-x + 30$
    D. $20x + 40$

16. The profit, P, for selling n units of a certain product is modeled by the equation $P = an^2 - c$, where a and c are constants. If the profit from selling 20 units is $185 and the profit from selling 8 units is $17, what is the value of c?
    A. .25
    B. .5
    C. 15
    D. 30

Calculator

17. An installation of a certain solar panel for a home costs $10,000. As a result, yearly energy costs decrease from $3,070 to $2,512. Solving for which inequality yields after how many years the savings exceed the installation costs?
    A. $10,000 > (3,070 - 2,512)x$
    B. $10,000 < (3,070 - 2,512)x$
    C. $10,000 - 2,512 > 3,070x$
    D. $10,000 - 3,070 < 2,512x$

18. The score in a game is calculated by subtracting the number of wrong answers from four times the number of right answers. A person who answers 30 questions earns 70 points. How many answers did the person answer correctly?

19. Mr. Dodds has s students in his class. If he gives each student 5 rocks, he will have 5 rocks left over. In order to give each student 6 rocks, he will need 19 more rocks. How many students are in his class?

20. If $5p - 1 \geq 9$, what is the least possible value of $p + 3$?
    A. 1
    B. 2
    C. 3
    D. 5

$$y \leq -10x + 28$$
$$y \leq 4x$$

21. In the system of inequalities above, what is the maximum possible value of y?

$$2x = a$$
$$x + y = 4a$$

22. If $0 < a < \frac{1}{5}$, find a possible value of y.

Week 3

$$R + .001A = 1.2$$

23. The formula above relates the reduction factor of a roof with its area, A, in square feet. If $R > .6$ and $A > 200$, which of the following gives all possible values of A?
    A. $100 < A < 200$
    B. $A > 200$
    C. $200 < A < 600$
    D. $200 < A < 1,000$

Food	Cost	Weight (pounds)
Bag of tilapia filets	$14	4
Bag of catfish filets	$21	3

24. A vendor has up to $500 to purchase on bags of tilapia and catfish filets. The total weight of the filets can be no more than 150 pounds. If he buys 10 bags of tilapia, what is the greatest number of bags of catfish filet he can buy to satisfy the requirements?

25. When designing a stairway, an architect can use the formula $2h + d = 25$ where h is the riser height, in inches, and d is the tread depth, in inches. If the height of a particular stairway must be at least 4 inches and the depth must be at least 7 inches, which of the following inequalities models all possible values of h?
    A. $h \geq 4$
    B. $h \leq 7$
    C. $4 \leq h \leq 7$
    D. $4 \leq h \leq 9$

26. A teacher has 200 red marbles and 121 blue marbles available for distribution. For a math lesson, each child needs a full set of marbles, which consists of 7 red marbles and 3 blue marbles. What is the greatest number of children who can receive a full set of marbles?

Week 3

27. 5 feet of green fabric and 3 feet of white fabric are needed to make each flag for a high school pep rally. Originally, the members of the school art department planned on purchasing the exact amount of fabric required to make 200 flags. To save money, they purchased green fabric in bulks of 15 feet and white fabric in bulks of 20 feet. The department bought just enough bulks to make 200 flags. How many unused feet of fabric will be left over when they purchase the fabric in bulk?

28. Each small box loaded into a van weighs 5 pounds and each large box weighs 10 pounds. If 200 boxes were loaded and their total weight was between 1150 pounds and 1165 pounds, inclusive, what is a possible number of small boxes that were loaded into the van?

29. $\frac{2}{3}$ of a cup of sweet potatoes has 76 calories. 1 cup of carrots has 52 calories. A certain 2-cup mixture of sweet potatoes and carrots has 135 calories. How many cups of carrots are in the mixture?
    A. .25
    B. .5
    C. 1.25
    D. 1.5

30. A plant grows 5 feet every three years. If the equation $a = \frac{5}{3}n$ models this situation, what does n represent?
    A. The number of years it takes the plant to grow 5 feet
    B. The number of feet the plant grown in 3 years
    C. The age of the plant, in years
    D. The height of the plant, in feet

Week 3

Week 4: Rates and Measurements

Calculator

1. 400 inches of wrapping paper are needed to completely wrap a small box. How many boxes of this size can be completely wrapped with 1,800 feet of wrapping paper?

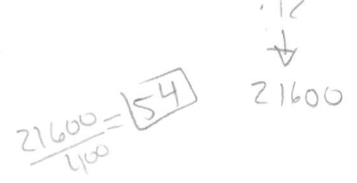

2. The ratio between the diameters of two pullies connected by a belt is $x:y$. The ratio of the revolutions per minute (rpm) of the two pullies is $y:x$. A smaller pulley has a diameter of 100 meters and a larger pulley has a diameter of 200 meters. If the rpm for the smaller pulley is 300, what is the rpm for the larger pulley?
   A. 100
   B. 150
   C. 300
   D. 600

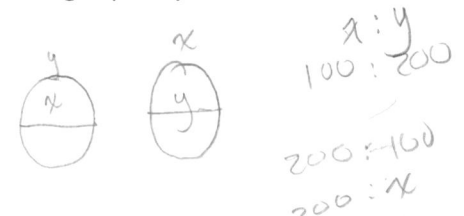

3. A toy car travels a distance of s inches in t seconds where $s = 15t^2$. Which of the following gives the speed of the car in inches per second?
   A. $15t$
   B. $15\sqrt{t}$
   C. $\frac{15}{t}$
   D. $\frac{15}{\sqrt{t}}$

4. 1 league is equivalent to 3 miles. 1 league is also equivalent to 960 rods. How many feet is 120 rods equal to? (5,280 feet = 1 mile)

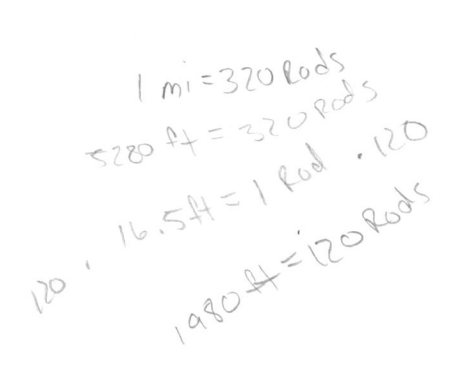

Week 4

5. 1 talent is equivalent to approximately 75 pounds. 1 pound is equal to 453.6 grams. Approximately how many kilograms are in 40 talents? (Round to the nearest whole number.)

   1t = 75 lb
   40 · 75 = 3000
   $$\frac{3000 \text{ lbs} \cdot 453.6g}{1000} = 1361 \text{ kg}$$

6. There are 660 feet in one furlong and 22 yards in one chain. How many chains are equivalent to 3 furlongs?

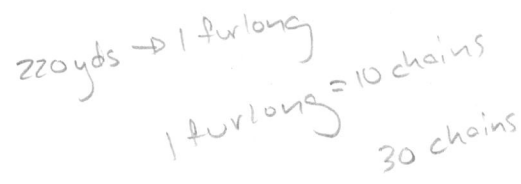

   220 yds → 1 furlong
   1 furlong = 10 chains
   30 chains

7. A certain car gets 30 miles to the gallon, and gas costs $3 per gallon. For a 200-mile trip, solving for which equation yields m, the number of miles driven that is equivalent to $24 worth of gas?
   A. $\frac{1}{10}m = 24$ ✓
   B. $\frac{1}{10}m = 176$
   C. $10m = 24$
   D. $10m = 176$

   $3 = 30 mi
   $1 = 10 mi
   $$\frac{\$1}{10 mi} = \frac{\$24}{m}$$

8. A car currently has 12 gallons of gas in its tank. Ty drives the car at an average speed of 50 miles per hour, and his car gets 27 miles to the gallon. Which function represents how many gallons remain in his tank after driving for h hours?
   A. $f(h) = 12 - \frac{27}{50}h$ ✓
   B. $f(h) = 12 - \frac{50}{27}h$
   C. $f(h) = 12 - \frac{h}{50 \times 27}$
   D. $f(h) = 12 - \frac{50 \times 27}{h}$

   12 - $\frac{27}{50}$·h

9. A car gets 25 miles to the gallon. If it is driven at a speed of 40 miles per hour, approximately how many gallons of gas are used after 3 hours of driving?
   A. 3
   B. 4
   C. 5 ✓
   D. 6

   $$\frac{120 mi}{25 mi} = 4.8$$

Week 4

10. Latisha drives a distance of 103.25 miles in 118 minutes. What was her average speed, in miles per hour?

$52.5 \frac{m}{h}$

11. Saoirse drives a distance of 18.4 miles from her school to her home at an average speed of 46 miles per hour. At this rate, how many minutes does it take her to drive from school to home?

$\frac{18.4}{46} \cdot 60 = 24$

Segment	Distance	Time
House to highway	5.2 miles	8.4 minutes
Highway to exit	6.8 miles	9.7 minutes
Exit to library	9.6 miles	17.9 minutes

12. Brett drives from his house to a library. The distance he traveled for each segment of the trip and the amount of time it took him to drive each segment are shown in the table above. What is Brett's average speed for the entire trip, in miles per hour?

13. A car travels a distance of 19.6 miles at a rate of 40 miles per hour. To the nearest whole number, how many minutes does it take the car to complete the trip?

14. A certain planet revolves 680,000,000 miles per year. Approximately how many miles does it revolve per hour?
    A. 78,000
    B. 99,000
    C. 1,863,000
    D. 28,000,000

Week 4

15. 139 people are enrolled in a self-study program for the bar exam. If the ratio of females to males enrolled in the program is approximately 4:3, which is closest to the number of males in the program?
    A. 35
    B. 59
    C. 80
    D. 104

16. The ratio of male to female rabbits in a forest is $18:81$. If there are 396 rabbits in the forest, how many are female?

17. If $x:y$ is $5:3$ and $y:z$ is $4:11$, what is the value $x:z$?
    A. 5:11
    B. 3:11
    C. 12:55
    D. 20:33

18. If the rise of a set of stairs is between 8 and 10 inches inclusive and the run is between 16 and 18 inches inclusive, which of the following could be the ratio between the rise and run?
    A. $\frac{1}{3}$
    B. $\frac{3}{5}$
    C. $\frac{2}{3}$
    D. $\frac{7}{9}$

19. A line includes the points (0,0), (3,9), and (a, b). If a and b are positive integers, what is the ratio of b to a?
    A. 9 to 1
    B. 3 to 1
    C. 1 to 3
    D. 1 to 9

Week 4

20. A graph (not shown) indicates that in a 60-day period, for every three days that passes, a certain tree planted in a plot grows two centimeters. What is the best interpretation of the slope of that graph?
    A. The ratio of the number of centimeters that the tree has grown since being planted to the number of days after which it has been planted
    B. The ratio of the number of days after which the tree has been planted to a height of 3 centimeters
    C. The ratio of the height of the tree, in centimeters, to its age, in days
    D. The ratio of the number of days passed to the distance between the top of the tree and the ground, in centimeters

21. A typist types at a rate of 300 characters per minute. Using the convention that 1 word equals 5 characters, how many words can the typist type in 3 hours?
    A. 3,600
    B. 1,500
    C. 10,800
    D. 270,000

22. The net productivity of a deciduous temperate forest is about 6,000 kilocalories per square meter in a year. A certain forest has a net productivity of 1.92×10^9 kilocalories per year. What is the approximate area of the forest, in square meters?
    A. 3.1×10^{-6}
    B. 3.2×10^5
    C. 1.2×10^{13}
    D. 2.4×10^{15}

23. A spacecraft submits a signal to Earth at a rate of 2×10^8 meters per second. If the spacecraft is 2.5×10^8 kilometers from Earth, approximately how many minutes does it take the signal to reach Earth?
    A. 1
    B. 21
    C. 48
    D. 75

Week 4

Week 5: Percents, Linear and Exponential Growth, and Graphs

Calculator

1. David's meal costs $4 more than Kelley's. Kelley's costs x dollars. If they tip 10% and split the cost, how much do they each pay?
   A. $.2x + .4$
   B. $.6x + 1.2$
   C. $1.1x + 2.2$ ←
   D. $2.2x + 4.4$

   $\dfrac{1.1(x+4+x)}{2} = 1.1\left(\dfrac{2x+4}{2}\right) \quad 1.1(x+2)$

2. Pairs of jeans cost $34.90 each and sweaters cost x dollars each. Inez buys 2 sweaters and one pair of jeans. The entire purchase is taxed 7.5%. If she spends d dollars, which expression models this situation?
   A. $d = 1.075(34.90 + 2x)$ ←
   B. $.075d = 34.90 + 2x$
   C. $1.075d = 34.90 + 2x$
   D. $d = .075(34.90 + 2x)$

   $(34.90 + 2x)1.075 = d$

3. 5 liters of a mixture containing 30% salt is mixed with another solution containing 60% salt. If the resulting mixture is 50% salt, how many liters are in the 60% solution?

   $0.3(5) + 0.6(x) = 0.2(5+x)$

   $1.5 + 6$

   $1.5 + 0.6x = 10 + 2x$

   $-8.5 = 1.4x \quad \boxed{x = 6.07}$

Budget	Percentage of Net Income
Housing (of this, 70% is rent and 30% is utilities)	45%
Food and Clothing	15%
Transportation	10%
Other (transportation, savings)	30%

4. Amy's monthly budget is shown above. Amy's budget is $n\%$ utilities. What is the value of n?

   $45 \cdot 0.3 \qquad 13.5\%$

Week 4

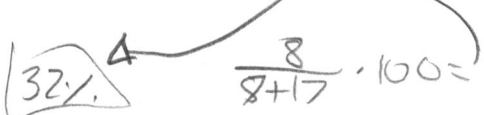

5. The ratio of red apples to green apples at a store is 8:17. What percent of these apples are red?

$\boxed{32\%}$ $\frac{8}{8+17} \cdot 100 =$

6. 40% of a class are males. 70% of the males and 82% of the females own at least one pet. To the nearest one decimal place, what percent of all students own at least one pet?

40 · 0.7 = 28   28 + 49.2 = $\boxed{77.2\%}$
60 · 0.82 = 49.2

7. 45% of the students in a school are males. If 40% of the males and 30% of the females take Italian, what percent of the people who take Italian are males? (Round to the nearest whole percent.)

0.40 · 45 = $\boxed{18}$

8. A toy costs d dollars after a 5% tax and a 30% discount. Which expression gives the value of the original price of the toy?
   A. $1.05(.7)d$
   B. $\frac{p}{(1.05)(.7)}$ $(x \cdot 0.7)1.05 = d$ $\frac{d}{1.05 \cdot 0.7}$
   C. $.75d$
   D. $\frac{p}{.75}$

(B circled)

9. The sum of three numbers is 1035. One number, x, is 30% more than the sum of the other two numbers. What is the value of x?

$\overbrace{a+b}$
$x + (x \cdot 1.3) = 1035$

$2.3x = 1035$ $\boxed{x = 450}$

10. An object costs $575.10 after a 25% discount and a second 10% discount. What was the original price, in dollars?

$(((x).75) \cdot .9) = 575.10$ $\frac{575.10}{0.75 \cdot 0.9} =$

0.75 · 0.9   9)12.86...

Week 5   38

11. How many liters of a 40% sugar solution must be added to 4 liters of a 10% sugar solution to make a 20% sugar solution?

12. Salt in a certain mixture has a mass of 69 grams. If the sample is 1.5% salt by mass, what is the mass of entire mixture, in grams?

Year	Price of Item
2010	$8,800
2011	$10,560

13. In the table above, the percent increase in the value of the item from 2010 to 2011 was double the percent increase from 2011 to 2012. What was the price in 2012?
   A. $11,088
   B. $11,616
   C. $12,672
   D. $14,784

14. John made $9 an hour for his first 10 hours of work. He will make $10 an hour for any additional hours of work he does later in the week. He saves 80% of his earnings. At least how many additional hours must he work to save $104?
   A. 3
   B. 4
   C. 13
   D. 14

Week 5

15. In a set of marbles, 40% are white, 20% are red, 15% are blue, and 30 are green. How many red marbles are in the set?

16. A printer prints at a constant rate. If 20% of 800 pages of a book are printed in 10 minutes, which equation models how many pages remain to be printed after t minutes?
    A. $y = 800(.8)^{t/10}$
    B. $y = 800 - .8t$
    C. $y = 800 - 16t$
    D. $y = 800 - 160t$

17. A sweater cost $72 after a 10% discount. What was its original price, in dollars?

18. A customer earns an 8% cash back bonus for the amount by which a purchase at a boutique jewelry store exceeds $2,000. All items at the store are worth at least $3,000. Which function models the value of the bonus for a purchase of d dollars?
    A. $C(d) = .08(d - 2000)$
    B. $C(d) = .08(d - 3000)$
    C. $C(d) = .08(2,000 - d)$
    D. $C(d) = .08(3,000 - d)$

19. The value of stock increased from $10 to $20. The value of the stock increased by what percent?
    A. 25%
    B. 50%
    C. 100%
    D. 200%

20. A mixture that is 15% sugar is mixed with one that is 30% sugar. The resulting mixtures contains 10 milliliters of solution and is 24% sugar. Which systems of equations could be used to model this situation?
    A. $x + y = 24$ and $.15x + .30y = 10$
    B. $x + y = 10$ and $.15x + .30y = .24$
    C. $x + y = 10$ and $.15x + .30y = 24$
    D. $x + y = 10$ and $.15x + .30y = .24(x + y)$

Week 5

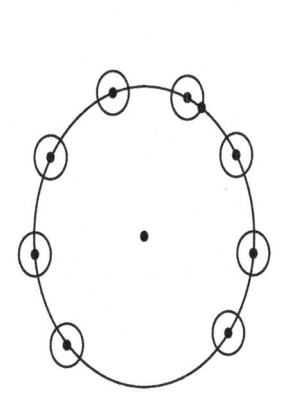

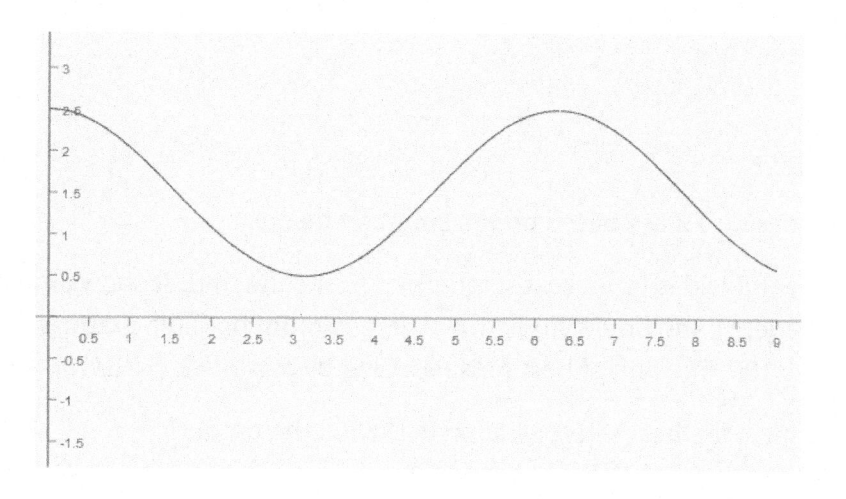

21. A toy Ferris wheel spins at a constant rate. The graph of the function $f(t)$ is shown above. What can $f(t)$ represent as a function of time?
   A. The distance of one seat from the center of the Ferris wheel
   B. The distance of one seat from the ground
   C. The speed of the Ferris wheel
   D. The acceleration of the Ferris wheel

22. Kalora deposits $50 into an account with an interest rate of 4.5% compounded annually. To the nearest <u>dollar</u>, how much money is in her account 10 years after she makes a deposit?

   $50 \cdot (1.045)^{10} = 77.6$

   $78

24. A company's revenue from sales triple each year since its founding. Which of the following types of models can best be used to depict its revenue?
   A. Linear, because revenue increases by a constant percent of its initial value
   B. Linear, because revenue increases by a constant percent of its current value
   C. Exponential, because revenue increases by a constant percent of its initial value
   D. Exponential, because revenue increases by a constant percent of its current value

25. Clara buys a blouse that is marked down by $\frac{1}{3}$ of its normal price of $60. She also buys a bag marked down by 20% of its normal price. She pays $103.68 for the blouse and bag, a price that includes an 8% tax. What is the normal price of the bag, in dollars?

Week 5

Week 6: Data I

Calculator

Questions 1 to 3 are based on the situation below.

A student decides to make a scatter plot (not shown) that shows the relationship between a test grade, y, and hours studied, x. The minimum possible grade is 0 and the maximum possible grade is 100. The line of best fit is modeled by $y = 47 + 5.25x$.

1. What is the best interpretation of 5.25 in the model?
   A. For every 5.25 hours one studies, one can expect to increase his or her grade by 1 point
   B. The actual score increase is 5.25 points per hour of studying
   C. The expected score increase is 5.25 points per hour of studying
   D. Every student who studies one hour will earn a score of 52.25

2. According to the line of best fit (20, 152) is a solution to the equation. What is the most likely interpretation of this result?
   A. A person who studies more than 20 hours will receive a perfect score
   B. It is impossible for a person to study for 20 hours
   C. The equation does not do a good job modeling results for someone who studied 20 hours
   D. A person cannot earn a perfect score without studying for a substantial number of hours

3. What is the best interpretation of the y-intercept in the equation of the line of best fit?
   A. The lowest grade one can possibly receive on the test
   B. The lowest score any student has ever managed to achieve on this test
   C. The score below which no student who does not study can earn
   D. A score close to that which a student who does no studying is likely to earn

Questions 4 and 5 are based on the scatter plot below, which shows the relationship between battery life and number of hours a phone is used for 13 different phones.

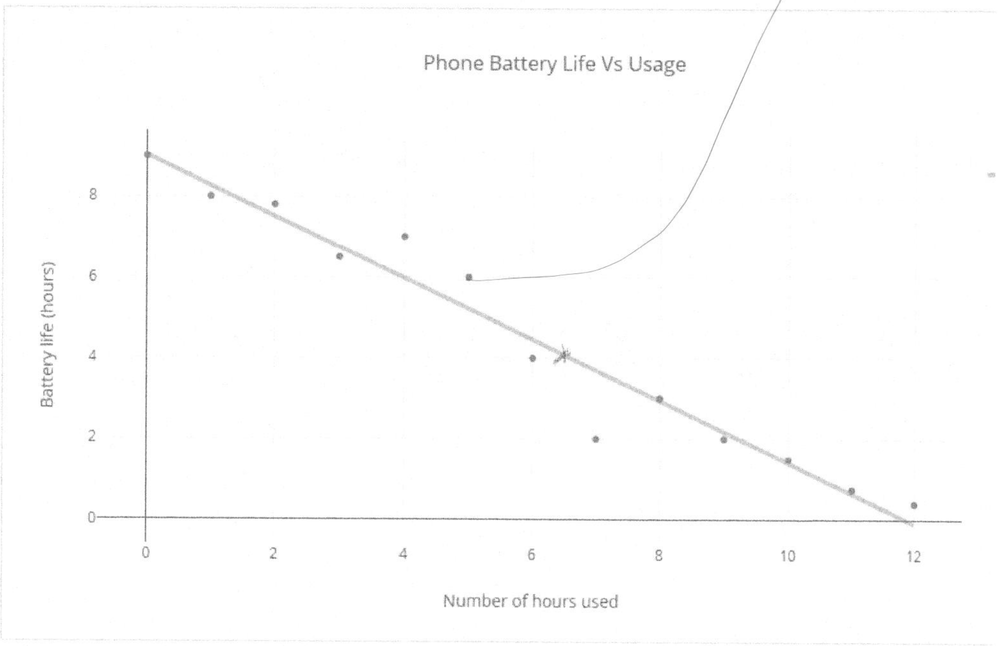

4. A certain phone has at least 4 hours of battery life. If this value is greater than that predicted by the line of best fit, what is the greatest possible number of hours that the phone is used?
   A. 0
   B. 1
   C. 5
   D. 6

5. For what fraction of the 13 data points on the scatter plot above does the line of best fit overestimate the battery life of the phone?

Questions 6 and 7 are based on the table below.

Production (in hundreds of units)

	Factory A	Factory B	Factory C
Widget P	20	40	30
Widget R	70	60	50

6. What fraction the widgets shown in the table were produced at Factory A?

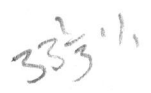

   $33\frac{1}{3}\%$

7. A widget from each factory shown in the table is selected random. Approximately how much more likely is the widget from Factory C to be Widget R than is the widget from Factory B to be Widget R?
   A. .83 times as likely
   B. 1.04 times as likely
   C. 1.11 times as likely
   D. 1.2 times as likely

Questions 8 to 10 are based on the table below, which shows how many people improved their overall average from grade 9 to grade 10 using two study programs.

Study Program	Improved Overall Average	Did Not Improve Overall Average
A	35	15
B	55	20

8. What is the probability that a person who used program A improved his or her overall average?
   A. $\frac{35}{50}$
   B. $\frac{35}{55}$
   C. $\frac{35}{90}$
   D. $\frac{35}{125}$

Week 7

9. A student from the table who did not improve is chosen at random. What is the probability the student used program B?

   A. $\frac{20}{35}$
   B. $\frac{20}{75}$
   C. $\frac{20}{90}$
   D. $\frac{20}{125}$

10. The percent of students who improved from program B is approximately how much greater than the percent who improved from program A? (Round to the nearest whole number.)

Questions 11 and 12 are based on the table below.

Preferred Genre	Preferred Style	
	Prose	Poetry
Fiction	7	9
Nonfiction	4	5

11. Given that a person from the table prefers prose, what is the probability that the person also prefers fiction?

12. Of the people who prefer nonfiction, what fraction prefer poetry?

Week 7

Wes rolled two dice at the same time 100 times and recorded whether each landed on an even number or an odd number. He recorded the results in the table below.

		Black die	
		Even	Odd
Red die	Even	28	23
	Odd	24	25

13. For what percent of the tosses did the red die land on an even number?

Mass and Volume of Material

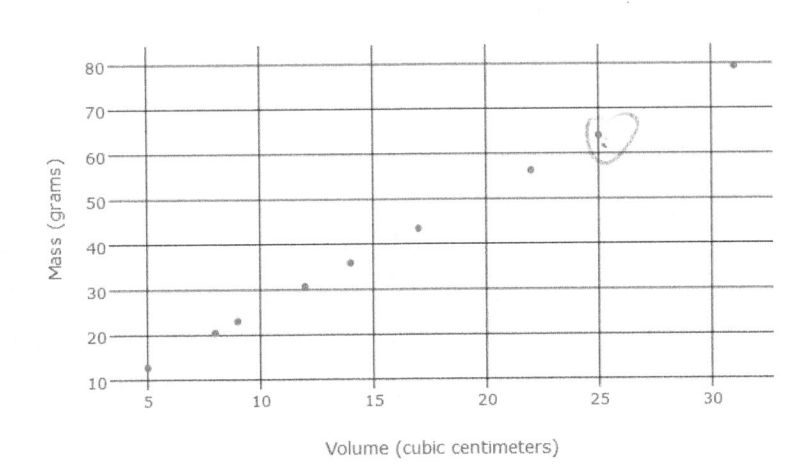

14. The mass of an object can be found by multiplying its volume by its density. The density of ivory is 1.84; the density of glass is 2.58; the density of red collar wood is .38; and the density of cast steel is 7.85. The object represented by the scatter plot above has a density closest to that of which of the following?

   A. Ivory
   B. Glass
   C. Red collar wood
   D. Cast steel

Week 7

Questions 15 to 17 are based on the scatter plot and the table below.

Weight and Mass of Objects on a Planet

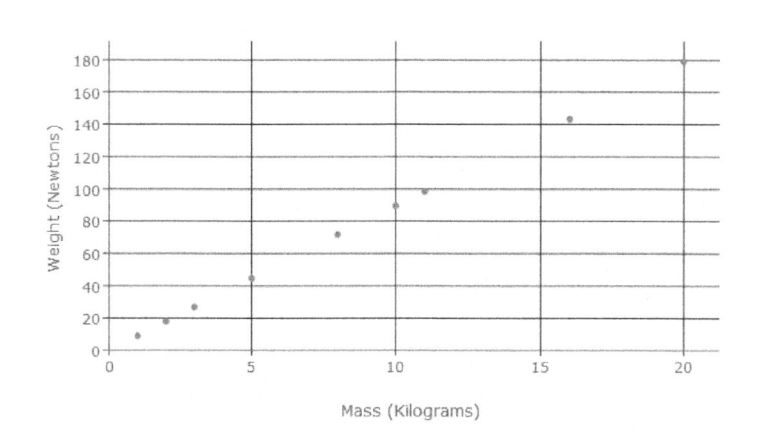

[Scatter plot with x-axis "Mass (Kilograms)" from 0 to 20 and y-axis "Weight (Newtons)" from 0 to 180]

Planet	Acceleration due to gravity (m/s²)
Mercury	3.7
Jupiter	23.12
Saturn	8.96
Neptune	11

The weight of an object in newtons is equal to the product of the mass in kilograms and the acceleration due to gravity in meters per second squared. The table above shows the acceleration due to gravity and the scatter plot shows the weight of objects of various masses.

15. Which planet is represented by the scatter plot?

    A. Mercury
    B. Jupiter
    C. Saturn
    D. Neptune

16. A line of best (not shown) is drawn to model the weight of the objects. What is the real-life meaning of the slope?

    A. The lowest possible weight of an object
    B. The maximum possible mass of an object
    C. The acceleration due to gravity
    D. The increase in mass as weight increases by 1 newton

Week 7

47

17. The equation $W = 9.8m$ can be used to find the weight of an of an object, in Newtons, on Earth with a mass of m kilograms. According to the table, an object weighing 49 Newtons on Earth weighs how many pounds on Neptune?

Flavor	First Grade	Second Grade
Chocolate	15	17
Vanilla	12	11
Strawberry	10	12
Pistachio	8	6
Rocky Road	5	2

18. In a scatterplot (not shown) of the data above, the flavor preferences of the first graders are shown on the x-axis and those of the second graders are on the y-axis. The line $y = x$ is drawn. How many of the 5 data points (each data point=one flavor) will appear above the line $y = x$?
    A. 1
    B. 2
    C. 3
    D. 4

Questions 19 to 21 are based on the table below.

The table below shows how three groups of adults scored on a trivia quiz.

	4 out 4	3 out of 4	2 out of 4	1 out of 4	0 out of 4	Total
Group 1	5	6	4	3	2	20
Group 2	7	6	3	3	1	20
Group 3	6	5	4	1	4	20
Total	18	17	11	7	7	60

19. Given that Dayna scored a 1, what is the probability she was in group 1 or 2?

20. What percent of the people in the three groups who took the quiz earned a score of 4?

Week 7

21. If a person scored at least a 2, what is the probability this person was in group 3?
A. $\frac{4}{11}$
B. $\frac{15}{20}$
C. $\frac{15}{46}$
D. $\frac{15}{60}$

Response	Frequency
Strongly Support	24
Moderately Support	72
Moderately Oppose	65
Strongly Oppose	19

22. The table above shows the views of 180 randomly selected voters from a city on their views on a measure to increase the budget of the public library for children's educational programs. If the sample is representative of the views of the city as a whole, and there are 300 thousand people in the city, how many more people are expected to strongly or moderately support the measure than strongly or moderately oppose the measure, in thousands? (Round to the nearest integer).

$$300{,}000\left(\left(\frac{96}{180}\right)-\left(\frac{84}{180}\right)\right)=20$$
(20,000)

Week 7

Week 7: Data II

Calculator

1. The average of the first 10 ratings of a product is 85 out of 100. What is the minimum score needed on the 11th rating for the average of the first 20 ratings to be a 92?

2. The average number of points scored by 6 players in a game is 24. When the highest player's score is removed, the average number of points scored by the remaining players is 19. How many points did the highest-scoring player earn?

3. The average of Nene's first four exams is a 90. What must she earn on the fifth test for an average of 91?

4. The average price of the cars at a certain dealership is $118,000, but the median price is $85,000. Which of the following is true?
   A. There an equal number of cars with values below $118,000 as there are above $118,000
   B. A small number of cars are valued much higher than the rest
   C. A small number of cars are valued much lower than the rest
   D. Most cars are valued between $85,000 and $118,000

Questions 5 and 6 are based on the situation below.

The table below shows how three groups of adults scored on a trivia quiz.

	4 out 4	3 out of 4	2 out of 4	1 out of 4	0 out of 4	Total
Group 1	5	6	4	3	2	20
Group 2	7	6	3	3	1	20
Group 3	6	5	4	1	4	20
Total	18	17	11	7	7	60

5. What was the average score of the adults in Group 2?

2.75

6. Which of the following best compares the median score between Groups 1 and 2?
    A. The median for Group 1 is higher
    B. The median for Group 2 is higher
    C. The medians for both groups are equal
    D. There is not enough information to determine the medians

	Density (grams per cubic centimeter)				
Sherilynn	1.7	2.9	1.8	3.6	4
Pippa	3	2.7	1.1	4.2	x

7. Sherilynn and Pippa collected five rocks, and their densities are shown above. If the average density of the rocks Pippa collected is 2 more than the density of those Sherilynn collected, what is the value of x?

8. If x is the average of p and 10 and y is the average of $3p$ and 14, what is the average of x and y?
    A. $p + 3$
    B. $p + 6$
    C. $2p + 12$
    D. $4p + 24$

$p + 10 = 2x$ $2y = 3p + 14$

$$\frac{\frac{4p+24}{2} = \frac{2p+12}{2} = p+6}{2}$$

Week 7

Class A	
Grade	Frequency
59 and below	2
60-69	3
70-79	3
80-89	3
90-100	2

Class B	
Grade	Frequency
59 and below	0
60-69	1
70-79	2
80-89	6
90-100	4

9. Which of the following is true about the data above, which shows how 26 students into two classes performed on a test?
   A. The standard deviation for the grades of Class A is higher.
   B. The standard deviation for the grades of Class B is higher.
   C. The standard deviations for the grades of both classes are equal.
   D. There is not information to determine the relationship between each class's standard deviation of grades

Week 7

Number of Representatives	Frequency
8	4
9	4
10	1
11	1
13	3
15	1
18	1
19	2
25	1
29	1
32	1
53	1

10. 21 states had 8 or more representatives in the United States of Representatives in 2013. What is the median number of representatives among these states?

    A. 10
    B. 11
    C. 13
    D. 15

11. The weights of four dogs are 10 pounds, 28 pounds, 42 pounds, and x pounds. The average weight is more than 30 pounds. Which inequality models this situation?

    A. $\frac{10+28+42}{3} + x > 30$
    B. $10 + 28 + 42 + x > 30$
    C. $\frac{10}{4} + \frac{28}{4} + \frac{42}{4} + x > 30$
    D. $10 + 28 + 42 + x > 4(30)$

Number of Extension Courses Taken	School A	School B
0	10	10
1	30	40
2	40	60
3	100	80
4	20	10

12. The number of college extension courses taken by 400 students at two high schools is shown above. What was the median number of extension courses taken?

Week 7

Model	Price
Model A	$10,200
Model B	$24,000
Model C	$13,600
Model D	$11,000
Model E	$13,200
Model F	$15,000

13. In the table above, what is the median price of the models?
    A. $12,100
    B. $13,200
    C. $13,400
    D. $13,600

14. In a random sample of 300 eels collected from a freshwater lake, less than 35% have 0 to 9 plates (bony scales). Which of the following is most likely to be accurate?
    A. Most species of fish in the lake have 9 or fewer plates
    B. Most eels in the lake have 9 or fewer plates
    C. About 35% of all species of fish in the lake have 9 or fewer plates
    D. About 35% of all eels in the lake have 9 or fewer plates

15. A poll predicts a candidate will receive 52% of the vote with a margin of error of 4±%. If there are 9,000 voters, what is the least number of votes the poll predicts the candidate will receive?

16. A study is conducted to determine citywide support for the construction of a public golf course. Among a random sample of 500 city residents who are golfers, 452 supported the construction of the golf course. Which of the following is true about the survey?
    A. It shows that most city residents support the construction of the golf course
    B. The survey did not include enough people who play golf
    C. The survey did not include enough residents from other cities
    D. The sample used in the survey displayed selection bias because it is not representative of the population being studied

Week 7

17. A ballot measure requires more than 50% of the votes to pass. A poll shows that support for the bill among likely voters is 49% with a margin of error of ±3%. Which of the following can be concluded?
    A. The ballot will only receive 49% of the vote
    B. The ballot will not pass with 46% of the vote
    C. The ballot will pass with 52% percent of the vote
    D. The results of the poll are too close to determine if the ballot will pass.

Measure	Percent Support	Margin of Error
A	55%	±4.5%
B	46%	±3%
C	47%	±4%
D	54%	±2%

18. A researcher conducts a poll to determine support for measures that will appear on the ballot in the next election. All ballots need to pass with more than half of the vote. If the polls are conducted at a 95% confidence level, about which measure's chance of passage can the researcher LEAST confidently draw a definitive conclusion?
    A. A
    B. B
    C. C
    D. D

19. As part of a study, researchers sent surveys to female nurses in South Korea. On average, those nurses who worked longer shifts had higher rates of obesity than those who worked shorter shifts. Which of the following can be concluded from the study?
    A. Long shifts cause female nurses in South Korea to become obese
    B. Long shifts cause female workers in all industries in South Korea to become obese
    C. There is a positive association between working long shifts and obesity among female nurses in South Korea, but it may not be a cause and effect relationship
    D. There is positive association between working long shifts and obesity among male and female nurses in all countries, but it is not a cause and effect relationship

Week 7

20. A researcher designs an experiment to test the effect of sight on flavor perception. A group of adult volunteers are randomly divided into two groups. Each group is given identical drinks. One group receives the drinks with a flavorless red dye and the other receives the same drinks but with a flavorless green dye. On average, those receiving drinks with the red dye were more likely to guess the flavor was cherry while those receiving drinks with the green dye were more likely to guess the flavor was lime. Which of the following can be concluded?
    A. The color of the drinks was the cause of the average differences between the flavor guesses, and the results can be generalized to all adults
    B. The color of the drinks was the cause of the average differences between the flavor guesses, but the results cannot be generalized to all adults since the subjects were volunteers
    C. No conclusions about cause and effect can be made, but there is a correlation between color and flavor that can be generalized to all adults
    D. No conclusions can be drawn from the experiment

Salary Level Class	Salary Range	Frequency
1	$15,000-$24,999	14
2	$25,000-$34,999	8
3	$35,000-$44,999	8
4	$45,000-$54,999	9
5	$55,000-$69,999	7
6	$70,000-$84,999	11
7	$85,000-$99,999	7
8	$100,000-$124,999	5
9	$125,000-$139,999	3
10	$140,000-$179,999	8
11	$180,000-$225,000	3

Mean Salary: $72,112

21. The salaries of a random sample of 83 employees at a college are shown in the table above, and the mean salary of all 83 employees is written under the table. Close to 68% of all the salaries are within one standard deviation of the mean, as in a normal distribution. Of the following choices, which of the following is closest to the standard deviation?
    A. $15,000
    B. $20,000
    C. $50,000
    D. $100,000

Week 7

22. A study found that 30% of Americans ages 12-17 play video games daily. The margin of error was 3.2%. Which statement about the margin of error is true?
    A. 3.2% of the people ages 12-17 inaccurately reported playing video games daily
    B. It is impossible that more than 33.2% of Americans age 12-17 play video games daily
    C. It is unlikely that less than 25% of the Americans ages 12-17 play video games daily
    D. The percent of Americans ages 12-17 who play video games daily is 33.2%

The table below shows the frequency of different grades on a quiz.

Grade	Frequency
55	1
60	2
65	2
70	3
75	5
80	6
85	9
90	7
95	4
100	2

23. Which plot best represents the data from the table above?

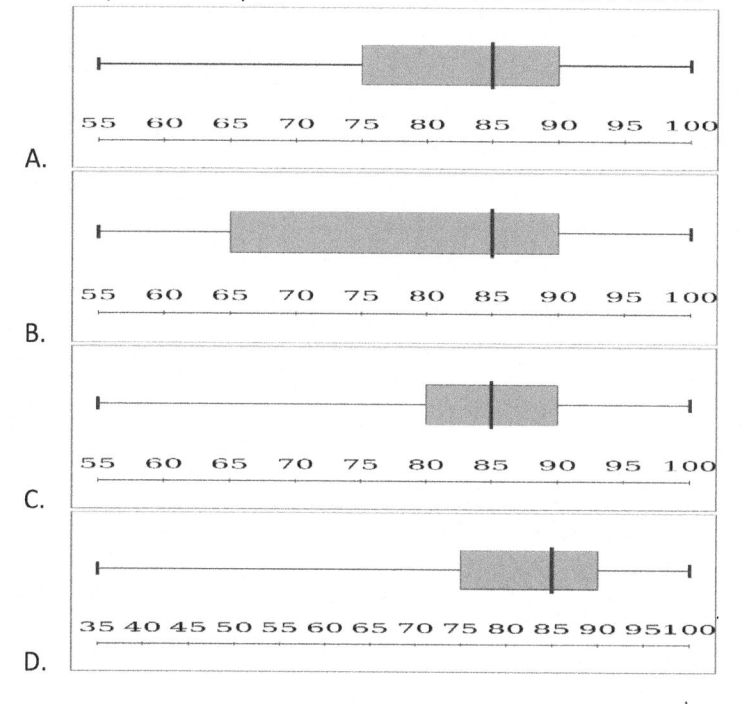

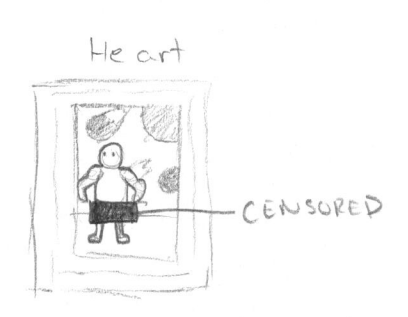

    A.
    B.
    C.
    D.

Week 7

24. In a certain study on the reading habits of high school students in a certain city, the margin of error for female respondents was 3.4% while the margin of error for male respondents was 4.2%. Which of the following is the most likely explanation for this difference?
    A. There are more males in the city than females
    B. Males were selected for the study by more biased methods
    C. The sample size was larger for males than for females
    D. The sample size was larger for females than for males

Week 8: Advanced Algebraic Operations

No Calculator

1. If $a - 3b = 10$, $\frac{3^a}{27^b}$ is equivalent to which of the following?
   A. 3^3
   B. 3^{10}
   C. 27^{10}
   D. It cannot be determined from this information.

   $\frac{3^a}{3^{3b}} = 3^{a-3b} = 3^{10}$

2. Which of the following is equivalent to $3^{\frac{3}{2}}$?
   A. $\sqrt[3]{3^2}$
   B. $\sqrt{3}$
   C. $3\sqrt{3}$
   D. $9\sqrt{3}$

   $\sqrt[2]{3^3}$
   $\sqrt[2]{3^2 \cdot 3}$
   $3\sqrt{3}$

3. Which of the following is equivalent to $8^{\frac{4}{5}}$?
   A. $\sqrt[4]{8}$
   B. $\sqrt[5]{8}$
   C. $\sqrt{2^{12}}$
   D. $\sqrt[5]{2^{12}}$

   $\sqrt[5]{8^4}$
   $\sqrt[5]{(2^3)^4} = \sqrt[5]{2^{12}}$

4. Which of the following is equivalent to $4^{\frac{3}{4}}$?
   A. $\sqrt[3]{4}$
   B. $\sqrt[3]{4^4}$
   C. $2\sqrt{2}$
   D. $4\sqrt{2}$

   $\sqrt[4]{4^3} \Rightarrow \sqrt[4]{(2^2)^3} = \sqrt[4]{2^6} = \sqrt[4]{2^4 \cdot 2^2} = 2\sqrt[4]{2^2} = 2 \cdot 2^{\frac{2}{4}} = 2 \cdot 2^{\frac{1}{2}} = 2\sqrt{2}$

   $16^{\frac{2}{4}} \Rightarrow 16^{\frac{1}{2}} = \sqrt{16} = 4$??

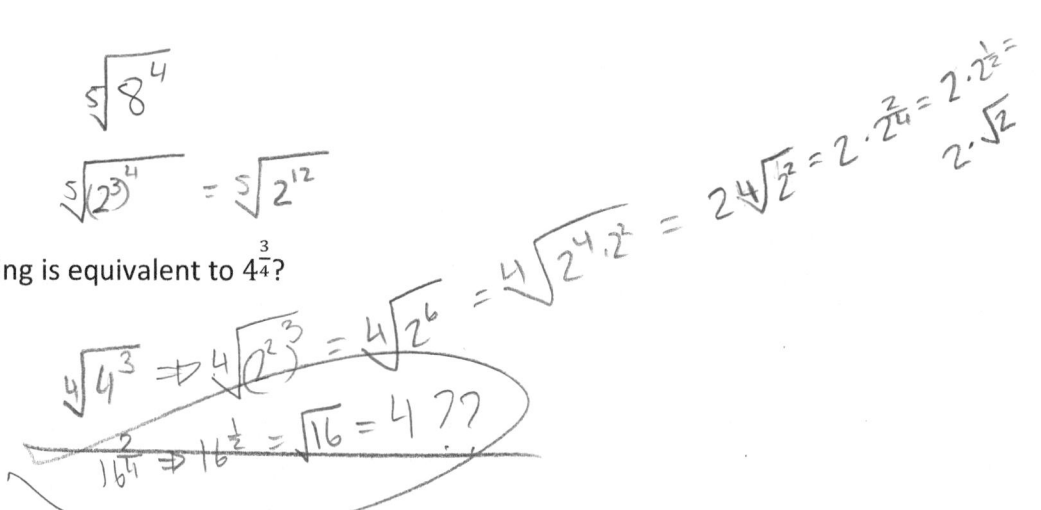

5. If $a > 1$ and $\sqrt[3]{a^7} \times \sqrt[4]{a^3} = a^n$, what is the value of n?
   A. $\frac{21}{12}$
   B. $\frac{33}{12}$
   C. $\frac{37}{12}$
   D. $\frac{38}{12}$

   $a^{\frac{7}{3}} \cdot a^{\frac{3}{4}} = a^{\frac{28}{12}} \cdot a^{\frac{9}{12}} = a^{\frac{28+9}{12}} = a^{\frac{37}{12}}$

6. If $a > 1$ and $\sqrt[5]{a} \times \sqrt[5]{a^9} = a^n$, what is the value of n?

7. Which of the following is equivalent to $(25x^2)^{\frac{1}{2}}$?
   A. $25x$
   B. $5|x|$
   C. $25|x|$
   D. $5x^2$

8. The expression $\dfrac{x^{-2}}{x^{\frac{1}{2}}y^{-3}}$ is equivalent to which of the following when x and y are greater than 1?
   A. $\dfrac{x^2}{\sqrt{xy^3}}$
   B. $\dfrac{\sqrt{x}}{y^3x^2}$
   C. $\dfrac{y^3}{x^2\sqrt{x}}$
   D. $\dfrac{y^3}{\sqrt[3]{x^2}}$

9. For all positive numbers x, $x^6 = 2$ and $x^{30} = n$. What is the value of n?
   A. $\sqrt[5]{30}$
   B. 5
   C. 10
   D. 32

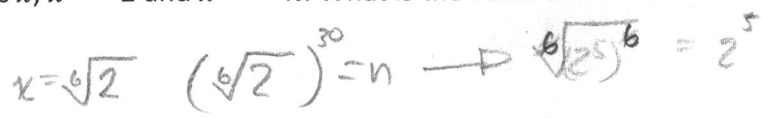

10. Which of the following is equivalent to $(a + \frac{b}{4})^2$?
    A. $a^2 + \dfrac{b^2}{4}$
    B. $a^2 + \dfrac{b^2}{16}$
    C. $a^2 + \dfrac{ab}{4} + \dfrac{b^2}{16}$
    D. $a^2 + \dfrac{ab}{2} + \dfrac{b^2}{16}$

Week 8

11. For all positive values of y, what is the value of n when $y^{\frac{1}{4}} \cdot y^2 = y^{\frac{n}{4}}$?
    A. 2
    B. 9
    C. 11
    D. 13

12. For all positive values of x and y, $(x^3y^4)^{\frac{1}{3}} \times (x^3y^4)^{\frac{1}{4}} = x^{\frac{n}{4}}y^{\frac{n}{3}}$. What is the value of n?
    A. 4
    B. 5
    C. 7
    D. 11

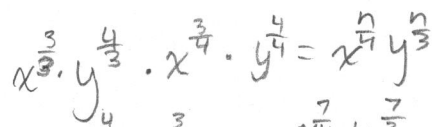

13. When $x > 1$ and $y > 1$, which of the following is equivalent to $\frac{x^3 y^{\frac{3}{2}}}{x^6 y}$?
    A. $x^3\sqrt{y}$
    B. $\frac{x^3}{\sqrt{y}}$
    C. $\frac{\sqrt{y^5}}{x^3}$
    D. $\frac{\sqrt{y}}{x^3}$

14. If $x = a^2 + 4b^2$ and $y = ab$, which of the following is equivalent to $4x + 16y$?
    A. $(2a + 4b)^2$
    B. $(a + 4b)^2$
    C. $(2a + 2b)^2$
    D. $(4a + 2b)^2$

$$(3x - 4)(x^2 + 2x + 5)?$$

15. Which of the following is equivalent to the expression above?
    A. $3x^3 + 2x^2 + 7x - 20$
    B. $x^3 - x^2 - 8x - 20$
    C. $3x^3 + 2x^2 + 23x - 20$
    D. $-4x^2 - 5x - 20$

Week 8

61

$$\frac{1}{2}x^2 - 5 = \frac{1}{2}(x-p)(x+p)$$

16. In the equation above, what is the value of p?
    A. $\sqrt{5}$
    B. $\sqrt{10}$
    C. 5
    D. 10

17. For all positive values of p and n, which of the following is equivalent to $\sqrt{(p-n)^3} \cdot \sqrt{(p-n)}$?
    A. $p - n$
    B. $p^2 - n^2$
    C. $p^2 - 2pn + n^2$
    D. $2p^2n^2$

18. If $f(x) = x^a$ for some positive constant a, and $f(16x) = 2f(x)$, what is the value of a?
    A. 4
    B. 2
    C. $\frac{1}{2}$
    D. $\frac{1}{4}$

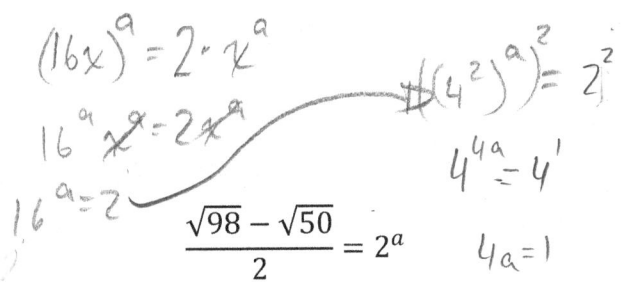

19. What is the value of a in the equation above?
$$\frac{\sqrt{98} - \sqrt{50}}{2} = 2^a$$

20. For $x > 1$, which of the expressions is equivalent to $(-2x^3)^{\frac{4}{3}}$?
    A. $-2x^4 \cdot \sqrt[3]{2}$
    B. $x^3 \cdot \sqrt[3]{16}$
    C. $2x^4 \cdot \sqrt[3]{2}$
    D. $2x^4 \cdot \sqrt[3]{16}$

Week 8

Calculator

21. Which of the following is an equivalent form of $\sqrt[4]{x^{12a}y^3}$ when $x > 1$ and $y > 1$?

    A. $x^{\frac{1}{3a}}y$

    B. $x^{3a}y^{\frac{3}{4}}$

    C. $x^{3a}y^{\frac{4}{3}}$

    D. $x^{4a}y^{-1}$

22. When x and y are positive numbers, which of the following must be equivalent to $(36x^{16}y^7)^{\frac{1}{2}}$?

    A. $6x^4y^{\frac{7}{2}}$

    B. $6x^{\frac{33}{2}}y^{\frac{15}{2}}$

    C. $18x^4y^{\frac{7}{2}}$

    D. $6x^8y^{\frac{7}{2}}$

23. If $(x^3)^2 = (x^{48})^n$ for $x > 1$, what is the value of n?

    A. $\frac{1}{8}$

    B. $\frac{1}{6}$

    C. $\frac{1}{4}$

    D. $\frac{1}{3}$

24. Which of the following is equal to $(1.6x - 2.2)^2 - (1.5x - 6.2)$?

    A. $1.6x^2 + 1.5x + 4$

    B. $1.1x^2 + 4.84x$

    C. $2.56x^2 - 8.09x - 1.8$

    D. $2.56x^2 - 8.54x + 11.04$

25. If $25x^4 - 9y^2 = 80$ and $5x^2 - 3y = 8$, what is the value of $5x^2 + 3y$?

Week 8

26. A company's costs are modeled by the equation $C = .10x^3 + .02x^2 + 2x + 10$ when x thousand items are sold. Sales can be modeled $S = 40 - .02x$ and revenue is modeled by $R = S \cdot x$. What is the profit, P, when x thousand items are sold and $P = R - C$?
   A. $.10x^3 + .04x^2 + 38x + 10$
   B. $-.10x^3 - .04x^2 + 38x - 10$
   C. $-.10x^3 + 40x + 10$
   D. $-.10x^3 + 38x - 10$

$$2x^3 + bx^2 + 6x + 3b$$

27. Which of the following must be a factor of the polynomial above when b is a constant?
   A. $3x + b$
   B. $2x + b$
   C. $2x^2 + 3$
   D. $x + 3$

$$\frac{1}{x^{\frac{b}{5}}}$$

28. In the expression above, b is a nonzero constant. If $x > 1$ and the expression is equivalent x^4, what is the value of $\frac{3b}{4}$?
   A. -20
   B. -15
   C. 10
   D. 20

29. If $n > 0$, which of the following is equivalent to $\sqrt[n]{3^{3n} \cdot 2^{n+5}}$?
   A. 432
   B. $54 + \sqrt[n]{32}$
   C. $54\sqrt[n]{32}$
   D. $1296\sqrt[n]{1776}$

Week 8

Week 9: Advanced Algebraic Operations II

No Calculator

$$f(x) = \frac{x^2 + 7x - 30}{x - 3}$$

1. The expression above is equal to $x + a$ when x is not 3. What is the value of a?

$$\frac{1}{\frac{1}{x-3} + \frac{1}{x+4}}$$

2. If $x \neq 3$ and $x \neq -4$, which of the following is equivalent to the expression above?
   A. $\frac{2x+1}{x^2+x-12}$
   B. $\frac{x^2+x-12}{2x+1}$
   C. $x^2 + x - 12$
   D. $2x + 1$

$$f(x) = x^3 - 16x$$
$$g(x) = x^2 - 7x + 12$$

3. Which of the following is equivalent to $\frac{f(x)}{g(x)}$ when $x > 4$?
   A. $\frac{1}{x+4}$
   B. $\frac{x+4}{x-3}$
   C. $\frac{x(x-4)}{x-3}$
   D. $\frac{x(x+4)}{x-3}$

$$\frac{24x^2 + 26x + 73}{ax - 1} = -12x - 7 + \frac{66}{ax - 1}$$

4. What is the value of a in the equation above?

    A. -3
    B. -2
    C. 2
    D. 3

5. If $\frac{48x^2+50x+15}{ax-1} = -24x - 13 + \frac{2}{ax-1}$, what is the value of a?

    A. -3
    B. -2
    C. 2
    D. 3

6. Which of the following is equivalent to $\frac{14x^2+18}{2x-4}$?

    A. $7 + \frac{2}{18}$
    B. $7x + 23$
    C. $7x + 14 + \frac{74}{2x-4}$
    D. $7x + 14 + \frac{23}{2x-4}$

$$\frac{3x^2 + 8x - 16}{16 - x^2}$$

7. Which of the following is equivalent to the expression above when $x \neq 4$ and $x \neq -4$?

    A. $-3 - \frac{16}{x-4}$
    B. $-3 + \frac{8}{-x+4}$
    C. $-3 + \frac{8}{x+4}$
    D. $3 + \frac{8}{x-4}$

Week 9

$$g(x) = 3x - 1$$
$$f(x) = 2 - g(x)$$

8. In the system of functions above, what is $f(0)$?

    A. -2
    B. -1
    C. 1
    D. 3

9. If $f(x - 3) = 7x + 10$, what is the value of $f(2)$?

x	$f(x)$	$g(x)$
1	3	-3
2	5	-3
3	-6	5
4	2	-1
5	3	0

10. For the table above, for what value of x does $f(x) + g(x) = x$?

    A. 1
    B. 2
    C. 3
    D. 4

$$\frac{3}{x-2} + \frac{6}{3(x-2)}$$

11. Which of the following is equivalent to the expression above when $x \neq 2$?

    A. $\dfrac{5}{x-2}$
    B. $\dfrac{9}{3(x-2)}$
    C. $\dfrac{7}{x-2}$
    D. $\dfrac{15}{x-2}$

Week 9

$$\frac{1}{\frac{1}{x+2}+\frac{1}{x+5}}$$

12. If $x \neq -2$ or -5, the expression above is equivalent to which of the following?

    A. $x^2 + 7x + 10$
    B. $2x + 7$
    C. $\frac{x^2+7x+10}{2x+7}$
    D. $\frac{2x+7}{x^2+7x+10}$

$$\frac{(x+5)+(x+2)}{(x+2)(x+5)} = \frac{2x+7}{x^2+7x+10}$$

13. If $a \neq -1$, what is the value of n when $\frac{2a+3}{(a+1)^2} - \frac{2}{a+1} = \frac{n}{(a+1)^2}$?

$2a+3 - 2a+2 = n$ (sic)
$5 = n$ (sic, should be 1)

Calculator

x	$f(x)$
0	-4
2	8
6	32

14. In the table above, what is the value of $f(3)$?

    A. 12
    B. 14
    C. 16
    D. 20

$2x - 4 \cdot 3$
$\cdot 2$

$6x - 4 = f(x)$

Week 9

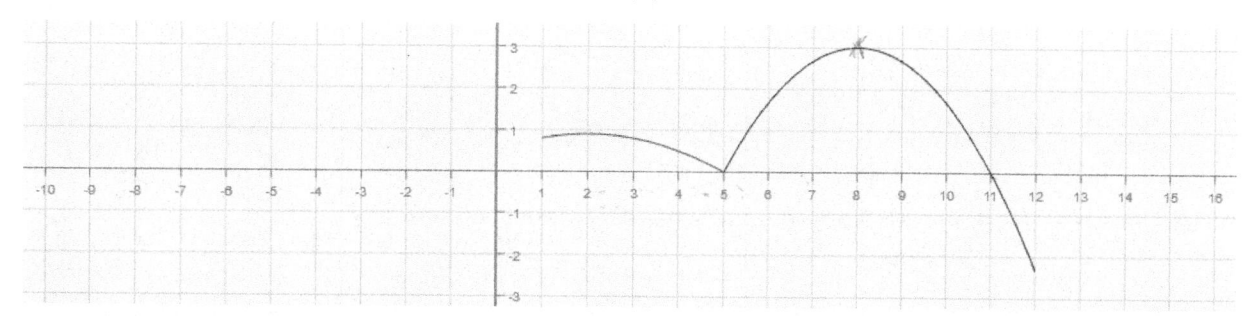

x	G(x)
2	4
3	1
4	9
5	2
6	3
7	5
8	7

15. The functions $F(x)$ and $G(x)$ are shown in the graph and table above, respectively. The maximum of $F(x)$ when $1 \leq x \leq 12$ is n. What is the value of $G(n)$?

   A. 1
   B. 3
   C. 7
   D. 8

16. A function g is defined by $g(n) = (n-2)(n+1)^3$. If $g(h-4) = 0$, what is one possible value of h?

17. The function $f(x) = (x+1)^2$. If $f(x+a) = x^2 - 8x + 16$, what is the value of a?

   A. -6
   B. -5
   C. -4
   D. 4

18. The function $f(x)$ has the coordinates (0,2) and (1,6). The slope of $g(x)$ is half that of $f(x)$ and $g(0) = 1$. What is $g(8)$?

Week 9

69

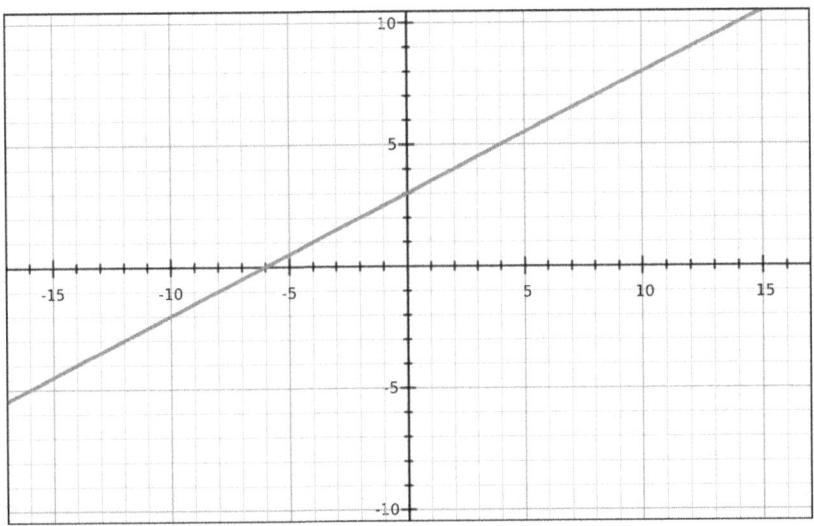

19. $g(x)$ has a slope that is four times that of $f(x)$, which is shown above. $g(x)$ includes the point $(0, -8)$. What is $g(10)$?

x	$f(x)$
1	3
2	5
3	7

20. In the table above, what is $f(100)$?

$$f(x) = \sqrt[3]{x}$$
$$g(x) = x^3$$

21. In the system of functions above, what is $f(g(-64))$?
   A. -64
   B. -4
   C. 8
   D. 64

Week 9

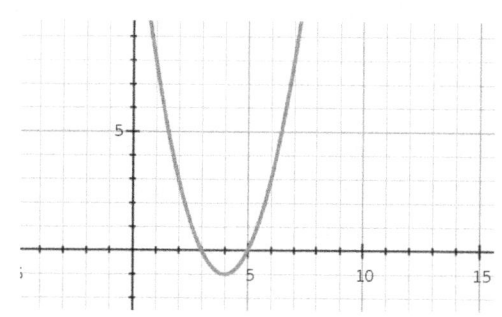

22. The function f is defined by $f(x) = x^2 - 4x + 3$. The graph of $y = f(x - h)$ is shown in the xy-plane above. What is the value of x?

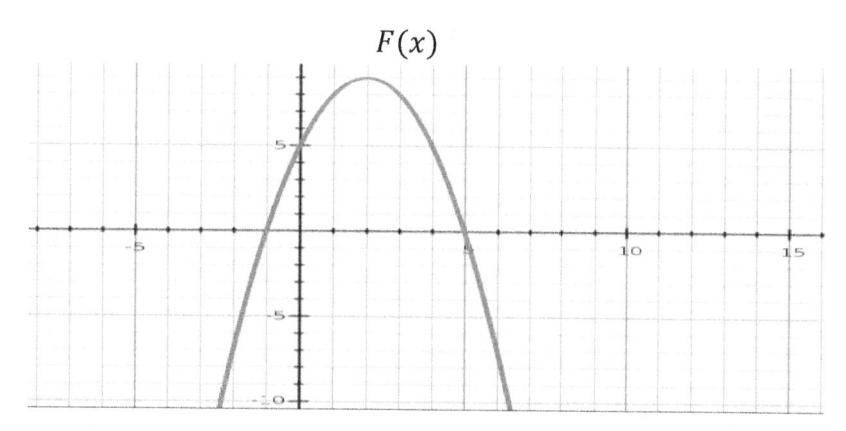

x	$G(x)$
-1	1
1	3
2	12
4	6

23. For what value of x on the table is $F(x) > G(x)$?

A. -1
B. 1
C. 2
D. 4

Week 9

$$f(x) = \frac{(x-a)^2 + 164}{2x}$$

24. In the function above, a is a positive constant. If $f(12) = 7$, what is the value of $f(6)$?

25. If $f(x) = 3x^2 - 7$ and $f(x+a) = 3x^2 + 12x + 5$, what is the value of a?
   A. -3
   B. -2
   C. 2
   D. 3

Week 9

Week 10: Advanced Algebraic Equations

No Calculator

1. If $2x^2 - 5x = p$ has no real solutions, which of the following is a possible value of p?
   A. -4
   B. -2
   C. 2
   D. 4

2. If $2x^2 + bx + 8$ has one real solution, what is the value of b if $b > 0$?

3. A polynomial can be written as $(p^2 - 4)(p + 3)^2$. What are all of the roots of the polynomial?
   A. 2 and -3
   B. 2, -3, and 4
   C. -2, 2, and 3
   D. -2, 2 and -3

4. $x^2 + \frac{k}{2}x + 4p = 0$. What are the possible values of x?
   A. $\frac{-k \pm \sqrt{k^2 - 64p}}{2}$
   B. $\frac{-k \pm \sqrt{k^2 - 64p}}{4}$
   C. $\frac{-k \pm \sqrt{k^2 - 4p}}{2}$
   D. $\frac{-k \pm \sqrt{k^2 - 4p}}{4}$

5. If $x^5 - 3x^3 + 2x = 0$, what is a possible integer value of x, if $x > 0$?

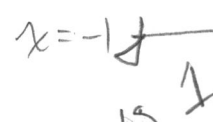

6. $(ax+3)(bx+7) = 18x^2 + cx + 21$ where a and b are constants and $a+b=9$. What are all possible values of c?
   A. 1 and 18
   B. 6 and 3
   C. 27 and 42
   D. 39 and 51

7. What is the solution set to $y = 3x^2 + 9x + 3$?
   A. $\frac{-3}{2} \pm \frac{\sqrt{5}}{2}$
   B. $-3 \pm \sqrt{5}$
   C. $-3 \pm \sqrt{2}$
   D. $3 \pm \frac{\sqrt{5}}{2}$

8. If $x(x^4 - 5x^2) = -4x$ and $x > 0$, what is a possible value of x?

$$x^3 - 6x^2 + 2x - 12 = 0$$

9. What is a possible integer value of x?

$$x - 3 = \frac{5}{x-3}$$

10. In the equation above, what is a possible value of $x - 3$?
    A. $\sqrt{5}$
    B. $\sqrt{5} - 3$
    C. $\sqrt{5} + 3$
    D. 5

Week 10

$$y = 16x^2 + bx + 64$$

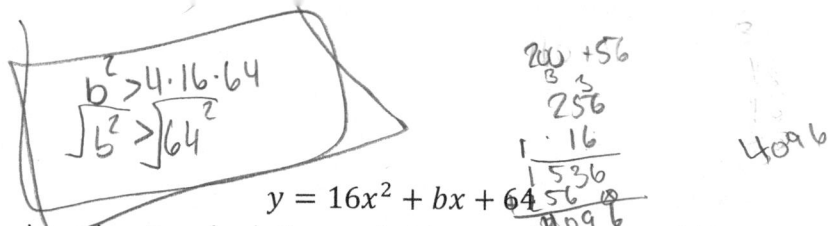

11. If the equation above has 2 real solutions, what is a possible value of b?
    A. -43
    B. -20
    C. 64
    D. 70

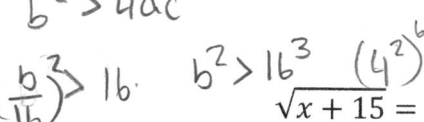

$$\sqrt{x+15} = x+3$$

12. What is the solution set to the equation above?
    A. {-6,1}
    B. {-6}
    C. {1}
    D. {-6,0,1}

13. If $\sqrt{x-5} = x-7$, which of the following is a solution?
    A. {6}
    B. {9}
    C. {6,9}
    D. {4,6}

$$\sqrt[3]{8r} = \frac{1}{2}r$$

14. If $r > 0$, what is the value of r in the equation above?

15. The graphs of $y = -18x^2 + 2$ and $y = 18x^2 - 2$ intersect at $(k, 0)$ and $(-k, 0)$. What is the value of k?
    A. $\frac{1}{9}$
    B. $\frac{1}{3}$
    C. 1
    D. 3

Week 10

75

16. If $y = a(x - 4)(x + 6)$ and (c, d) is the vertex of the parabola, which of the following is equivalent to d?
    A. $-a$
    B. $-2a$
    C. $-16a$
    D. $-25a$

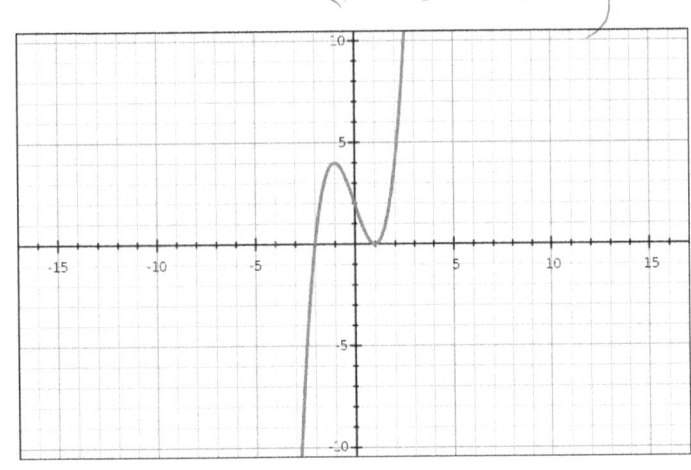

    $x^2 - 4x + 6x - 24$
    $x^2 + 2x - 24 + 1 - 1$
    $a(x+1)^2 - 25 = y$

17. What is the equation of the polynomial above?
    A. $y = (x - 1)(x + 2)$
    B. $y = (x + 1)(x - 2)$
    C. $y = (x - 1)^2(x + 2)$
    D. $y = (x + 1)^2(x - 2)$

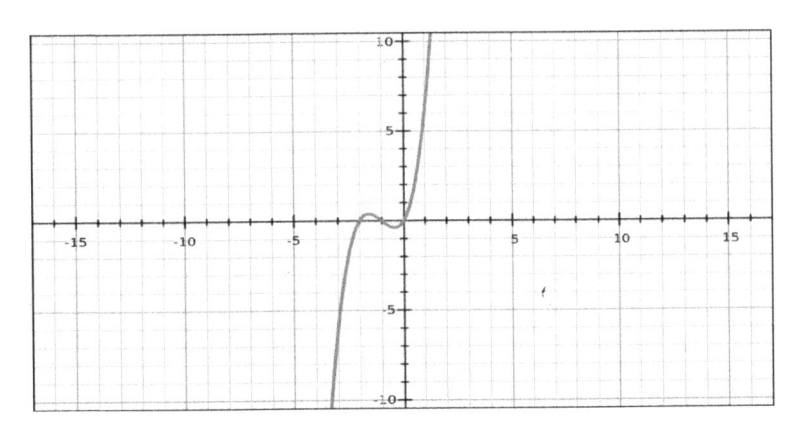

    $(x+2)(x-1)^2$

18. What is the equation of the function above?
    A. $y = x^3 + 3x^2 + 2x$
    B. $y = -x^3 - 3x^2 - 2x$
    C. $y = x^3 + 2x^2 - x - 2$
    D. $y = -x^3 - 2x^2 + x + 2$

    $(x+2)(x+1)\,x$
    $x^3 + 3x^2 + 2x$

Week 10

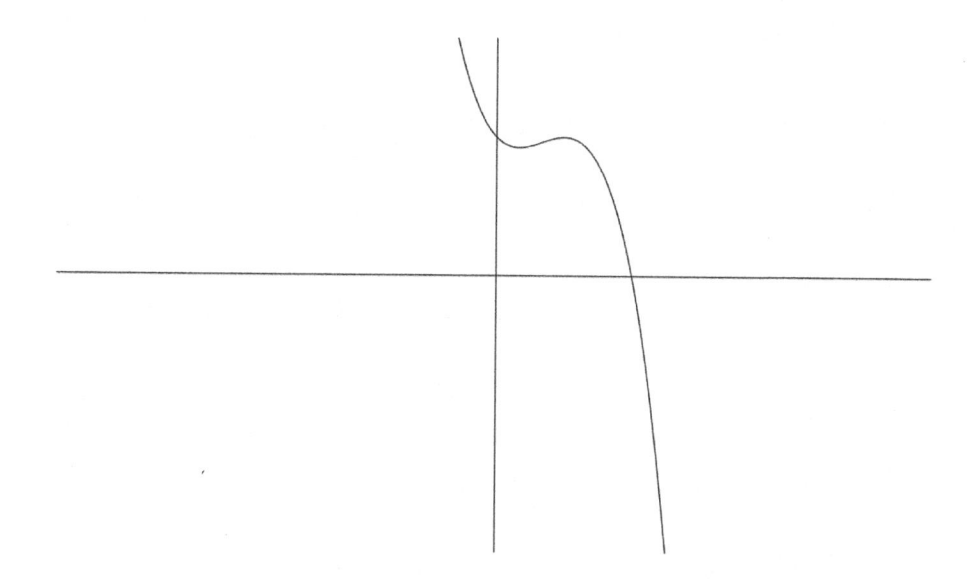

19. Which of the following could be the equation of the graph shown above?
    A. $y = (x^2 + 1)(x + 2)$
    B. $y = (x - 1)^2(x + 2)$
    C. $y = (x^2 + 1)(x - 2)$
    D. $y = (x^2 + 1)(2 - x)$

20. In the equation $y = (x + 2)(x - 8)$, what is the x-coordinate of the parabola's vertex?

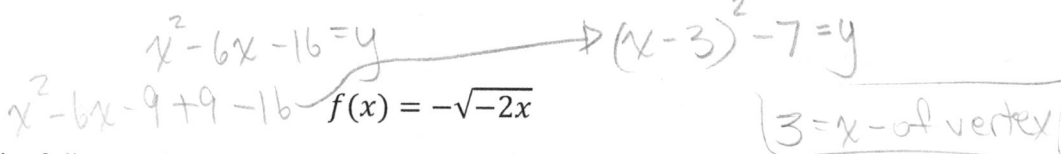

$$f(x) = -\sqrt{-2x}$$

21. Which of the following best defines the domain of the function above?
    A. All real numbers
    B. All real numbers except 0
    C. All real numbers greater than or equal to 0
    D. All real numbers less than or equal to 0

22. The expression $(x - a)(x + a)(x - b)$ can be written as $x^3 - 3x^2 - 16x + t$. What is the value of t?
    A. 4
    B. 16
    C. 48
    D. 96

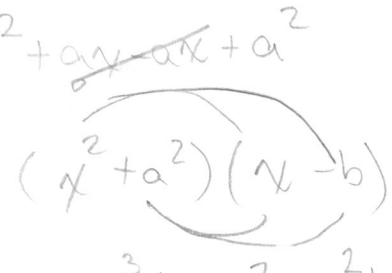

Week 10

77

23. If $\sqrt{xy+2} = 3$, what is the value of x^2y^2?

24. If $x^2 + y^2 = 13$, what is the value of $x^4 + 2x^2y^2 + y^4$?

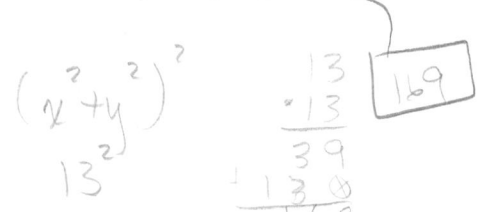

25. If $4a - 12b = 20z$, which if the following is equivalent to $a^2 - 6ab + 9b^2$?
    A. $\frac{1}{5}z$
    B. $\frac{1}{5}z^2$
    C. $5z^2$
    D. $25z^2$

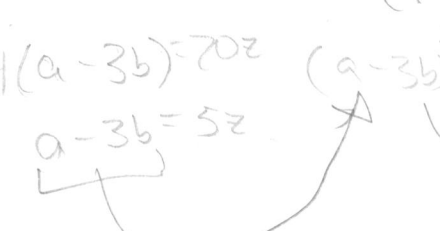

Calculator

26. If $\sqrt{x-b} = 4b$ and $b < 0$, which of the following is true about the equation?
    A. No values of x satsify the equation
    B. x has exactly 1 solution
    C. x has exactly 2 solutions
    D. There is not enough informaion to determine if there is a solution for x

27. Which of the following is true about the graph of $y = -2(x-3)^2 + 7$
    A. The vertex is (3,7) and the graph opens upward
    B. The vertex is (3,7) and the graph open downward
    C. The vertex is (3,7) and the graph opens upward
    D. The vertex is (-3,7) and the graph opens downward

Week 10

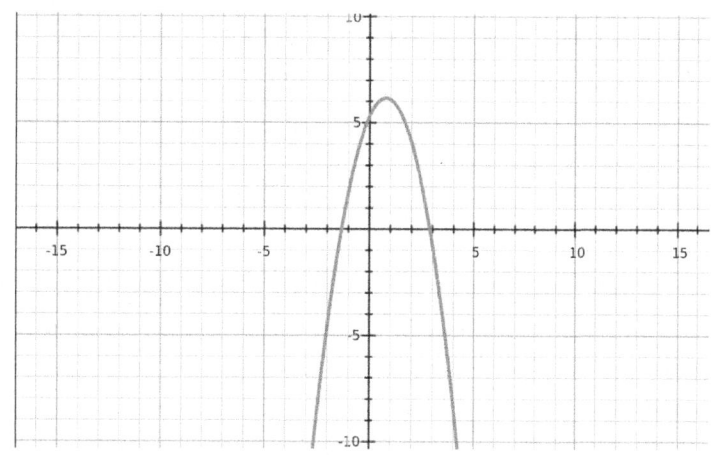

28. What is the equation of the parabola shown above?
   A. $y = 1.4x^2 + 2.2x + 5.3$
   B. $y = -1.4x^2 + 2.2x + 5.3$
   C. $y = 1.4x^2 - 2.2x + 5.3$
   D. $y = -1.4x^2 + 2.2x - 5.3$

29. For the equation $y = (x+5)(x+3)$, which interval contains the x-coordinate of the vertex?
   A. $-5 < x < -3$
   B. $-2 < x < 1$
   C. $3 < x < 5$
   D. $4 < x < 8$

$$f(x) = (x-2)(x^2 - 6x + 8)$$

30. How many distinct zeros does the function above have?
   A. Zero
   B. One
   C. Two
   D. Three

31. Which of the following is an example of a function with no x-intercepts?
   A. A quadratic equation with one real zero
   B. A quadratic function with two real zeros
   C. A line with a positive slope
   D. A cubic function with no real zeros

Week 10

32. Which of the following is the equation of a graph with no x-intercepts?
    A. $y = 3x$
    B. $y = x^2 - 6x - 7$
    C. $y = x^2 + 2x + 8$
    D. $y = 2x^3 + 4x^2 + 3x + 6$

33. Which of the following reveals the y-intercept(s) of a parabola as (a) constant(s) or coefficient(s)?
    A. $x = y^2 - 2y - 8$
    B. $x = (y - 4)(y + 2)$
    C. $y = \sqrt{x + 9} + 1$
    D. $x + 9 = (y - 1)^2$

34. Which of the following reveals the x-intercept(s) of a parabola as (a) constant(s) or coefficient(s)?
    A. $x = y^2 - 2y - 8$
    B. $x = (y - 4)(y + 2)$
    C. $y = \sqrt{x + 9} + 1$
    D. $x + 9 = (y - 1)^2$

$$y = \frac{4x + 8}{3x^2 + 6x + 3}$$

35. Which of the following is an equivalent form of the rational function above such that the values not included in the domain are shown as constants or coefficients?
    A. $y = \frac{2x+4}{x^2+2x+1}$
    B. $y = \frac{4(x+2)}{3x^2+6x+3}$
    C. $y = \frac{4x+8}{3(x^2+2x+1)}$
    D. $\frac{4x+8}{3(x+1)(x+1)}$

36. In which equation is the vertex of the parabola farthest from the x-axis?
    A. $y = (x - 6)(x + 2)$
    B. $y = .5(x - 6)(x + 2)$
    C. $y = 2(x - 6)(x + 2)$
    D. $y = -10(x - 6)(x + 2)$

Week 10

37. There are originally 100 male rabbits and 150 female rabbits in a study. Then another 100 female rabbits are added to the study. How many male rabbits must be added to the study in order for the male rabbits to be $\frac{1}{3}$ of all the studied rabbits?

Week 11: Advanced Quadratics and Polynomials

No Calculator

1. What is the distance between the coordinates in the solution set of $y = 49$ and $y = (x-2)^2$?

    A. 4
    B. 5
    C. 7
    D. 14

$$x = 2y + 1$$
$$y = (2x - 1)(x + 2)$$

2. How many ordered pairs satisfy the systems of equations above?

    A. 0
    B. 1
    C. 2
    D. Infinitely many

3. The graph of the function f is defined by $f(x) = -\frac{1}{2}(x-6)^2 + 5$ and the graph of the function g is defined by $g(x) = -4x + 5$. If $f(a) = g(a)$, what is a possible value of a?

$$x^2 + y^2 = 153$$
$$4x = y$$

4. If $x < 0$ in the system of equations above, what is the value of y?

    A. -24
    B. -12
    C. -8
    D. -4

5. If $6x - 2$ is factor of $18x^2 - cx + 5$, what is the value of c?

x	$f(x)$
0	7
2	5
3	0
4	1

6. In the table above, what is the remainder when $f(x)$ is divided by x?

7. For the function p, $p(1) = 3$. Which of the following must be true?
   A. $x - 1$ is a factor of $p(x)$
   B. The remainder when the function is divided by $x - 3$ is 1
   C. The remainder when the function is divided by $x - 1$ is 3
   D. The remainder when the function is divided by $x + 1$ is 3

8. If $x - 3$ is a factor of $y = x^3 - 2x^2 - cx + 3$, what is the value of c?

$$f(x) = 2x^3 - x^2 + 1$$
$$g(x) = -x$$

9. If $2x - 1$ is a factor of the function $p(x)$, which of the following can equal $p(x)$?
   A. $f(x)$
   B. $g(x)$
   C. $2f(x) + g(x)$
   D. $f(x) + 2g(x)$

Week 11

$$f(x) = 2(x^2 + 3x + 1) + 5(3x + k)$$

10. If $x + 1$ is a factor of the function above, what is the value of k?

Questions 11 and 12 are based on the figure below.

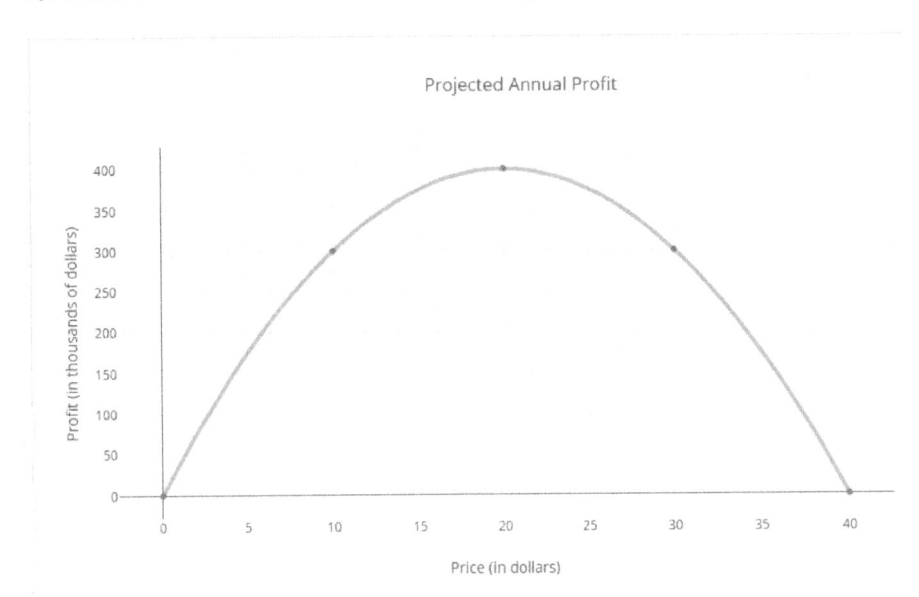

11. If the price per unit is x dollars, which of the following is a factor of the profit function shown above?

    A. $x - 20$
    B. $x - 40$
    C. $x + 40$
    D. $x - 400$

12. $p(x)$ is the quadratic function representing the graph shown above. Which of the following must be true about $p(x)$?

    A. $x - 10$ is a factor of $p(x)$
    B. When $p(x)$ is divided by $x - 10$, the remainder is 300
    C. When $p(x)$ is divided by $x - 300$, the remainder is 10
    D. When $p(x)$ is divided by $x + 10$, the remainder is 300

Week 11

$$y = ax^2 + n$$

13. In the equation above, a and n are positive constants. How many times does the graph represented by the equation above intersect the graph represented by the equation $y + 2n = -a$?

    A. None
    B. One
    C. Two
    D. Infinitely many

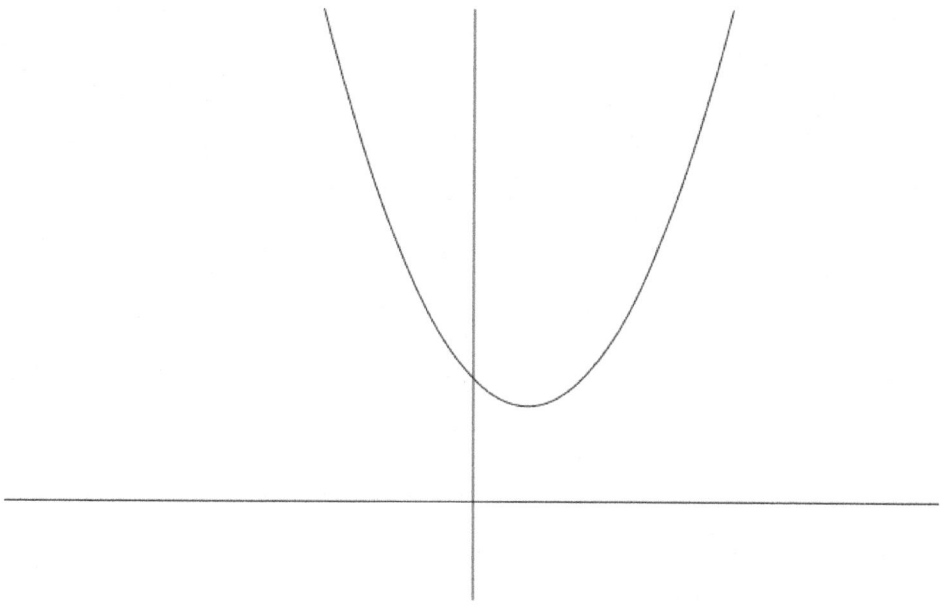

14. The graph above has the equation $y = 2x^2 + bx + 5$. Which of the following could be the value of b?

    A. -7
    B. -3
    C. 0
    D. 10

Week 11

Calculator

15. Friends plan to evenly divide the cost of a $200 gift for a teacher. When one more friend contributes, each friend pays $10 less than they otherwise would. How many friends <u>originally</u> planned to pay for the gift?

16. A trip costs $600 when divided evenly between x friends. After one friend backs out, each remaining friend pays $30 more. How many friends <u>originally</u> planned to split the cost of the trip?

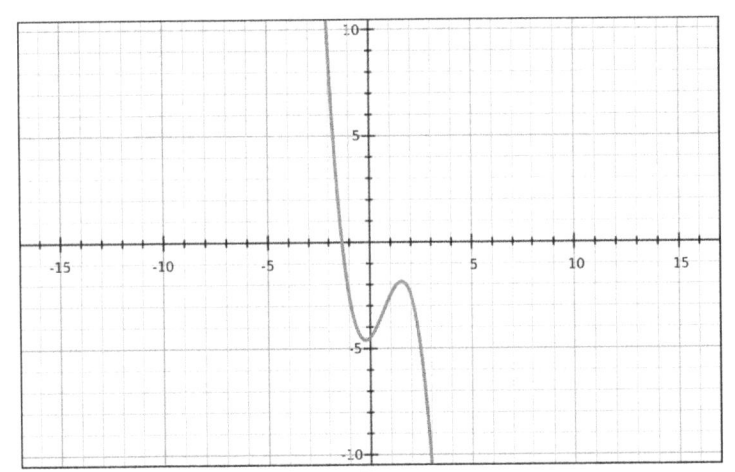

17. The function $f(x) = -x^3 + 2x^2 + x - 4.5$ is shown above. If $f(x) = k$ has three real solutions, what could be the value of k?
    A. -5
    B. -4
    C. -1
    D. 0

Week 11

18. The length of a rectangle is 8 feet more than its width. The area of the rectangle is 105 square feet. What is the <u>perimeter</u> of the rectangle, in feet?

19. When a shirt costs $24, 20 shirts are sold. When the price decreases by $2, 5 more shirts are sold. What price, in dollars, should be charged to maximize the revenue?

Questions 20 to 22 are based on the situation below where h is the height of a ball, in feet, thrown in the air t seconds after it is thrown.
$$h = -16t^2 + 40t + 110$$

20. From what height, in feet, is the ball initially thrown?

21. After how many seconds does the ball reach its maximum height?

22. To the nearest foot, what is the maximum height of the ball?

23. The formula $y = -\frac{1}{24}(x - 46)^2 + 48$ relates miles per gallon, y, to speed, x, in miles per hour of a certain vehicle. According to the model, at what speed, in miles per hour, does the car get its maximum gas mileage?

$$y = -x^2 + 2x + 7$$
$$y - 1 = x$$

24. What are all the solutions to the systems of equations above?
    A. (3,4)
    B. (-4,1) and (4,3)
    C. (-2,-1) and (3,4)
    D. (2,7) and (-4,-3)

Week 11

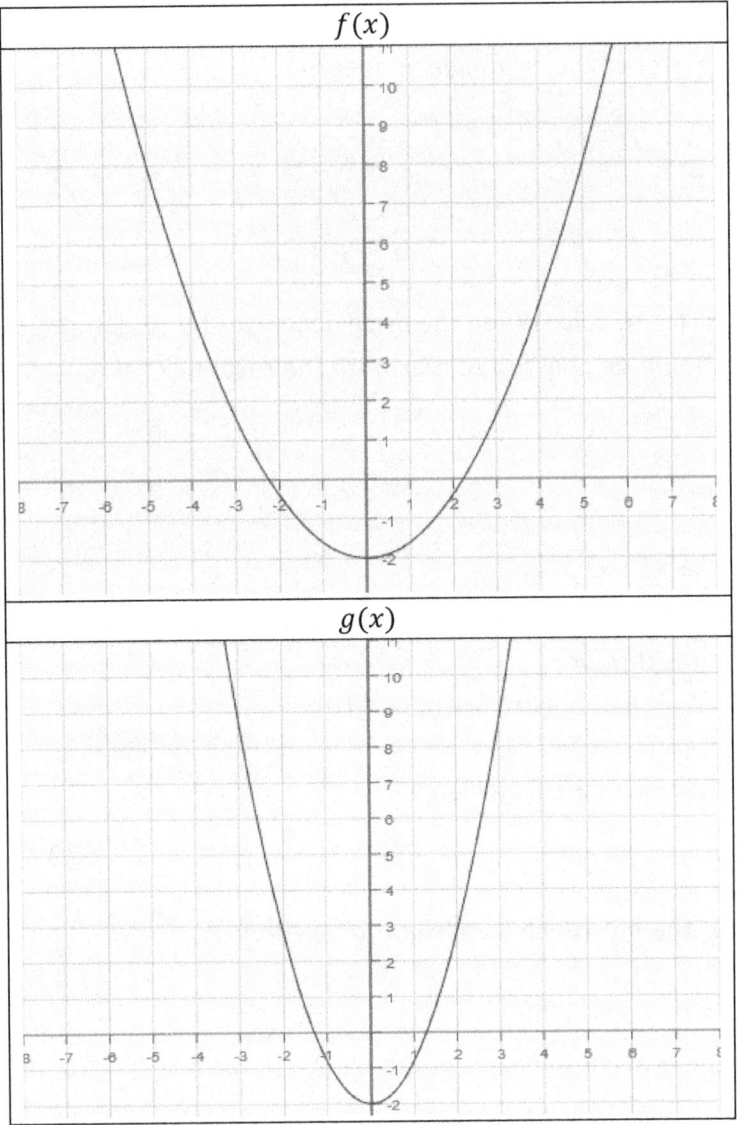

25. In the figures above, the graph of $f(x) = cx^2 - 2$ and the graph of $g(x) = dx^2 - 2$. Which of the following best expresses the relationship between the constants c and d?

A. $c = d$
B. $c > d$
C. $c < d$
D. There is not enough information to determine the relationship

Week 11

88

26. If the length of a rectangle is 5 more than its width and the length is x, which expression represents the area of the rectangle?
    A. $x^2 + 5$
    B. $x^2 - 5$
    C. $x^2 + 5x$
    D. $x^2 - 5x$

27. If $2(x^2 + ax) + 4(ax^2 + 3x) = bx$, what is the value of b?

Week 12: Exponential Functions in Context and Manipulating Expressions

No Calculator

1. The popluation of a city is 3 million. Since 1985, its population has grown by .13% each year. Which of the following models the population, P, in millions, t years after 1985?
   A. $P = 3(1.0013)^t$
   B. $P = 3(1.013)^t$
   C. $P = 3 + 1.3t$
   D. $P = 3 + 1.03t$

Question 2 is based on the function below.
$$f(x) = 2^x + 2$$

2. Which is a coordinate on the graph of $-f(x)$?
   A. (0,2)
   B. (0,-2)
   C. (0,3)
   D. (0,-3)

3. The number of people in a town decreases by 20% every 3 years. If there are 50,000 people in the town now, which function represents the number of people in the town in n years?
   A. $f(n) = 50,000(.2)^{3n}$
   B. $f(n) = 50,000(.8)^{3n}$
   C. $f(n) = 50,000(.2)^{\frac{n}{3}}$
   D. $f(n) = 50,000(.8)^{\frac{n}{3}}$

$$S = 2000(1.05)^t$$

4. The equation above models the number of subscribers, S, that a magazine has t years after its founding. Which of the following best models how many subscribers the magazine has q quarters after its founding?
   A. $S = 2000(1.0005)^q$
   B. $S = 2000(1.05)^{4q}$
   C. $S = 2000(1.05)^{\frac{q}{4}}$
   D. $S = 2000 + .0125q$

Week 12

5. The number of bacteria in a colony doubles every four minutes. If there are originally 50 bacteria, which of the following equations models the number of bacteria in the colony after x hours?

   A. $y = 50(2)^{\frac{x}{4}}$
   B. $y = 50(2)^x$
   C. $y = 50(2)^{15x}$
   D. $y = 50(2)^{240x}$

6. If $BC = AB + A$, which of the following is equivalent to B in terms of A?

   A. $A - C$
   B. $\frac{A}{C-A}$
   C. $\frac{C+A}{A}$
   D. $\frac{A}{C+A}$

7. If $3\sqrt{4x} = n$, what is the value of $4x$ in terms of n?

   A. $\frac{n}{9}$
   B. $\frac{n^2}{3}$
   C. $\frac{n^2}{9}$
   D. $9n^2$

8. The number of cells in a culture triples every 16 minutes. If there are originally 4 cells in the culture, which of the following equations models how many cells, y, are in the culture after h hours?

   A. $y = 4(3)^h$
   B. $y = 4(3)^{16h}$
   C. $y = 4(3)^{\frac{15h}{4}}$
   D. $y = 4(3)^{4h}$

9. If $\frac{a-b}{b} = \frac{4}{9}$, then which of the following must be true?

   A. $\frac{a}{b} = \frac{-4}{9}$
   B. $\frac{a}{b} = \frac{13}{9}$
   C. $\frac{a+b}{b} = \frac{13}{9}$
   D. $a - 4b = 13$

Week 12

10. If $\frac{x}{y} = x + z$, what is x in terms of y and z?

    A. $x = \frac{yz}{1-y}$
    B. $x = \frac{yz}{1+y}$
    C. $x = \frac{1+y}{z}$
    D. $x = \frac{1-y}{z}$

11. If $a, b,$ and c are positive integers and $4a^2 b^2 c^2 = 64$, what is the value of $9abc$?

Questions 12 and 13 are based on the situation below.

The average cost, in thousands of dollars, of homes in a community each year since 2005 is modeled by the equation $432(1.025)^x$.

12. What is the best interpretation of 432 in context?
    A. The estimated cost of each house x years after 2005
    B. The average housing cost in 2005
    C. The amount by which the housing cost increases each year since 2005
    D. The average housing cost each year since 2005

13. The average housing cost in 2008 is estimated to be how many times greater than the average housing cost in 2006?
    A. 1.025
    B. 1.025^2
    C. 864
    D. 432^2

14. The profits of a corporation, in millions, can be modeled by the exponential equation $P = 150(1.07)^{\frac{t}{4}}$, where t is the number of years since 2000. How many months does the model predict it will take to increase profits by 7%?
    A. 4
    B. 12
    C. 48
    D. 96

Week 12

Calculator

Questions 15 and 16 are based on the situation below.

The value of a stock decreases by 44% each year. The value of the stock after t years is given by the formula $y = 800(r)^t$.

15. What is the value of r?

16. What is the value of the stock after two years? (Round to the nearest dollar.)

17. Joseph deposited x dollars into an account in the year 2000. Each year the amount of money in his account doubled until he had $560 in 2003. What is the value of x?

18. A graph with the equation $y = ax^b$ where a is positive and b is negative has a graph that is
    A. a line with a negative slope
    B. a line with a positive slope
    C. an increasing exponential function
    D. a decreasing exponential function

$$k = \frac{1}{2}mv^2$$

19. The equation above relates kinetic energy, in joules, to mass, in kilograms, and velocity, in meters per second. Two cars have identical masses but the velocity of one car is three times that of the other. If the kinetic energy of the slower car is 30,000 joules, what is the kinetic energy of the faster car, in joules?
    A. 10,000
    B. 30,000
    C. 90,000
    D. 270,000

Week 12

$$S = 2xy$$
$$V = \frac{1}{5}Sy$$

20. In the equations above, for all positive values of x, y, S, and V, what is the value of x in terms of y and V?

    A. $x = \frac{2y^2}{5V}$
    B. $x = \frac{5y^2}{2V}$
    C. $x = \frac{5V}{2y^2}$
    D. $x = \frac{2V}{5y^2}$

$$q = \frac{1}{2}nv^2$$

21. The formula above relates the dynamic pressure, q, of a fluid to its velocity, v, and constant of density, n. Which of the following shows velocity in terms of dynamic pressure and constant of density?

    A. $v = \sqrt{\frac{2q}{n}}$
    B. $v = \frac{\sqrt{2q}}{n}$
    C. $v = 2qn$
    D. $v = \sqrt{\frac{2n}{q}}$

$$x = \frac{\sqrt{yz}}{20}$$
$$x = \frac{4+y}{60}$$

22. Based on the equations above, in which x, y, and z are positive integers greater than 1, which of the following is equivalent to $\sqrt{yz}$?

    A. $\frac{4+y}{3}$
    B. $\frac{3}{4+y}$
    C. $3(4+y)$
    D. $\frac{4+y}{1200}$

Week 12

23. (c, d) is a coordinate on the line $y = 3x + b$ and $(2c, 3d)$ is a point on the line $y = 4x + b$. What is the value of $\frac{c}{d}$, if $d \neq 0$?

Day	Number of bacteria in culture
1	1.5×10^5
2	3×10^5
3	6×10^5

24. The number of bacteria in a culture increases exponentially, as shown in the table above. At this rate, on what day would the number of bacteria reach closest to 1.536×10^8?
    A. Day 7
    B. Day 9
    C. Day 10
    D. Day 11

Time (minutes)	Temperature (Degrees Celsius)
0	205
5	149
10	110
15	82
20	63
25	50

25. The table above models the temperature of a dish t minutes after it has been removed from the oven. Which equation best models the relationship between its temperature in Celsius, C, and t?
    A. $C = 185 - 11.2t$
    B. $C = 185 - 7.8t$
    C. $C = 20 + 185(.93)^t$
    D. $C = 20 + 205(.93)^t$

Week 12

26. The formula for the period of a spring is given by the formula $T_s = 2\pi\sqrt{\frac{m}{k}}$, where m is the mass attached to the spring and k is the spring constant. If the period is doubled and the spring constant does not change, what is the ratio of the mass attached to the spring with the larger period to the mass attached to the spring with the smaller period?

A. 2 to 1
B. 4 to 1
C. 8 to 1
D. 16 to 1

Week 12

Week 13: Angles and Polygons

No Calculator

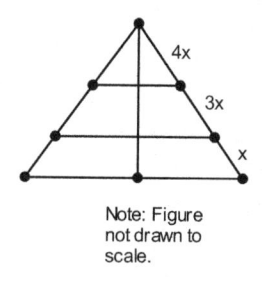

Note: Figure not drawn to scale.

1. A triangular shelf system with three parallel levels is shown above. If the height of the entire structure is 32 feet, what is the height of the middle level, in feet?

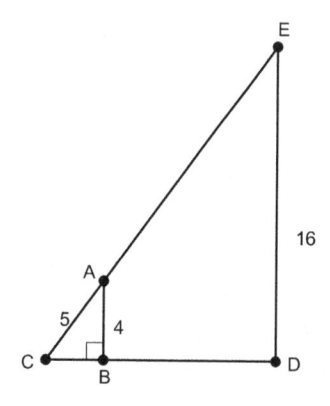

2. In the figure above, AB is parallel to DE. What is the length of BD?

Week 13

3. An isosceles triangle has one side length of 10. What is the greatest possible perimeter of the triangle, if all side lengths are integers?
   A. 31
   B. 39
   C. 40
   D. 41

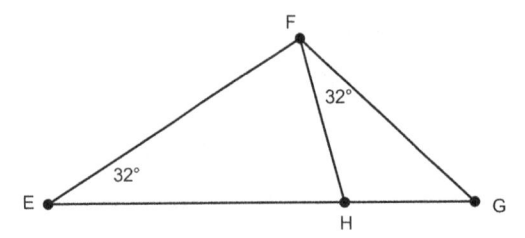

4. In the figure above, which of the following has the same value as $\frac{HG}{FH}$?
   A. $\frac{FG}{EF}$
   B. $\frac{EF}{FG}$
   C. $\frac{EH}{FG}$
   D. $\frac{FG}{EH}$

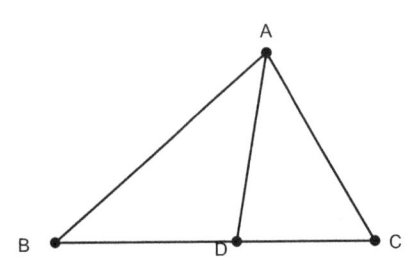

5. If AD bisects angle BAC, which of the following must equal $BD:DC$?
   A. $AC:AB$
   B. $AB:AC$
   C. $AB:AD$
   D. $DC:AC$

Week 13

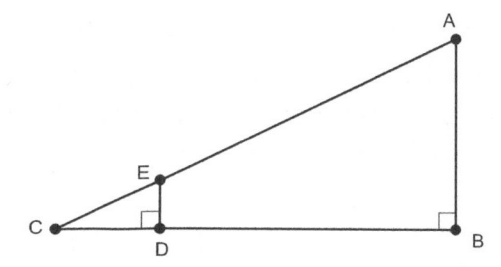

6. In the figure above, ED is parallel to AB, and CD is one third the length of BD. If $ED = 2$, what is the length of AB?

7. The length of a rectangular rug is l feet. The width is 4 feet shorter than its length. Which of the following expresses the perimeter of the rug, in feet, in terms of l?
    A. $l - 4$
    B. $2l - 4$
    C. $2l - 8$
    D. $4l - 8$

8. A right triangle with one angle measuring 30 degrees has a perimeter of $12 + 4\sqrt{3}$. What is the length of the longest side of the triangle?

Calculator

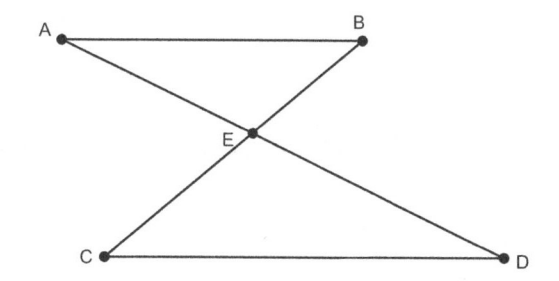

9. In the figure above, AD and CB intersect at E, AB is parallel to CD, $AB = 30, CD = 40$, and $AD = 49$. What is the length of AE?

Week 13

10. An artist bends a rod into the shape of a square. Another artist bends a rod of the same length into the shape of an equilateral triangle. The length of each side of the triangle is 3 feet more than that of the square. What is the area of the square, in square feet?

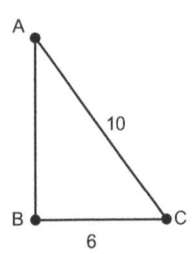

11. Triangle DEF (not shown) is similar to triangle ABC such that vertices D, E, and F correspond to vertices A, B, and C. Angles B and E are right angles. If $DE = 24$, what is the area of DEF?
    A. 108
    B. 216
    C. 384
    D. 432

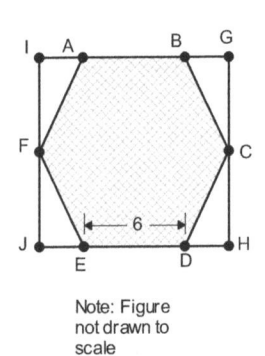

12. In the figure above, with regular hexagon ABCDEF within rectangle IGHJ, what is the area of rectangle IGHJ?
    A. $72\sqrt{3}$
    B. 81
    C. $81\sqrt{3}$
    D. 144

Week 13

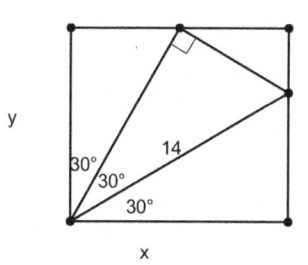

13. What is the area of the rectangle above, in square units?
    A. 49
    B. $49\sqrt{3}$
    C. $73.5\sqrt{3}$
    D. $105\sqrt{3}$

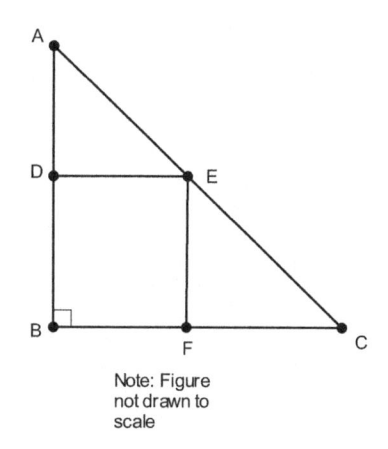

14. In right triangle ABC above, BDEF is a square, and $AB:BC = 3:4$. The area of square BDEF is what fraction of the area of triangle ABC?
    A. $\frac{24}{49}$
    B. $\frac{12}{25}$
    C. $\frac{9}{16}$
    D. $\frac{3}{4}$

15. A triangle has sides of 3, 4, and 6. Which of the following is true about the triangle?
    A. It is a right triangle
    B. It is an acute triangle
    C. It is an obtuse triangle
    D. No such triangle exists

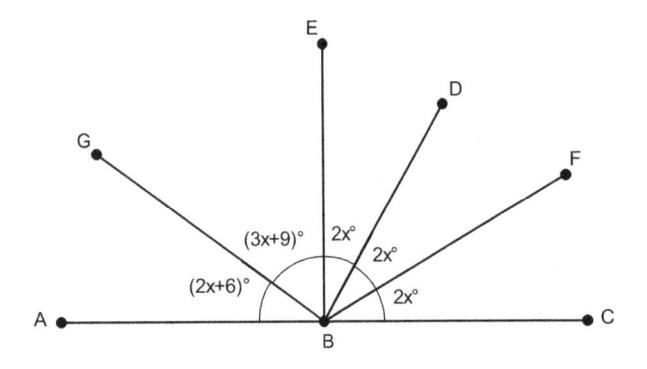

16. What is the measure of angle ABG, in degrees?

Questions 17 and 18 are based on the figure below.

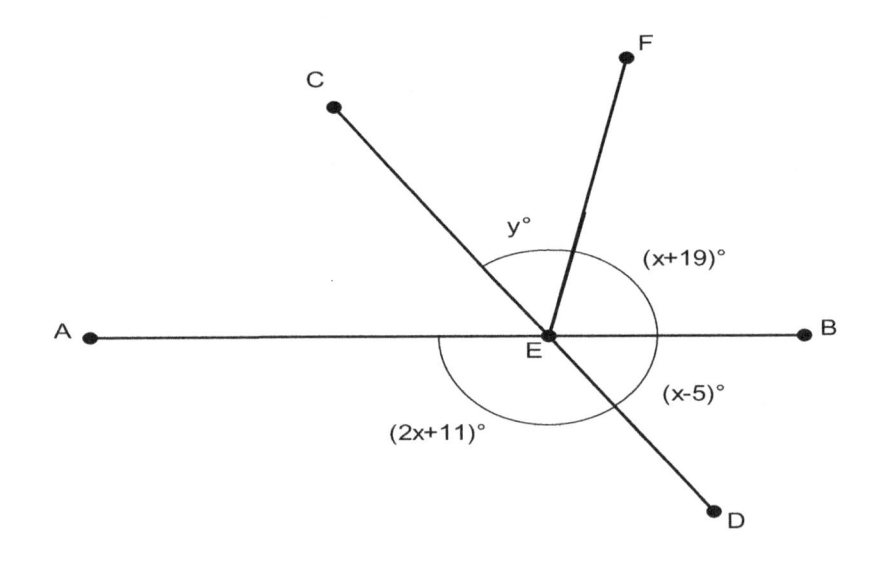

17. What is the value of x?

18. What is the value of y?

Week 13

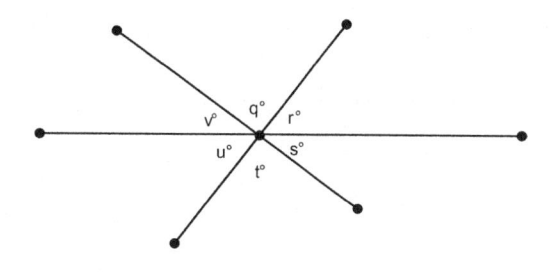

Note: Figure not drawn to scale.

19. If $q + r = s + t$, which of the following is NOT necessarily true?
    A. $q = t$
    B. $r = s$
    C. $u = s$
    D. $v = t$

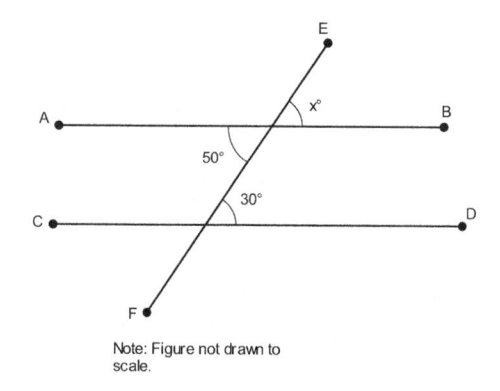

Note: Figure not drawn to scale.

20. The figure above shows segment AB of line k, segment CD of line m, and transversal EF. Which of the following must be true?
    A. Angle x measures 150 degrees
    B. Angle x measures 30 degrees
    C. Lines m and k are parallel
    D. Lines m and k intersect

Week 13

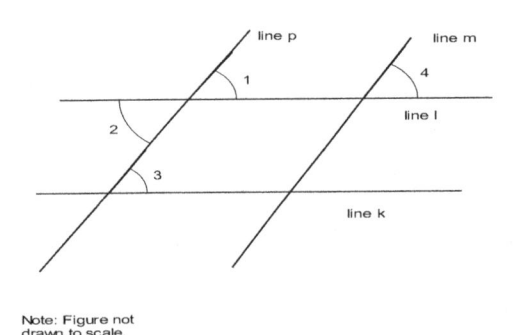

21. In the figure above, angles 1 and 3 both measure 50 degrees. Which of the following must be true?
    A. Angle 2 measures 130 degrees
    B. Lines p and m are parallel
    C. Lines l and k are parallel
    D. Lines l and k intersect

Questions 22 and 23 are based on the figure below.

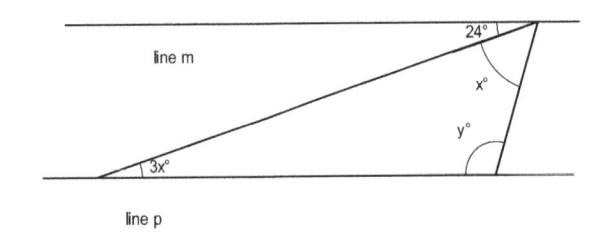

In the figure above, line m is parallel to line p.

22. What is the value of x?

23. What is the value of y?

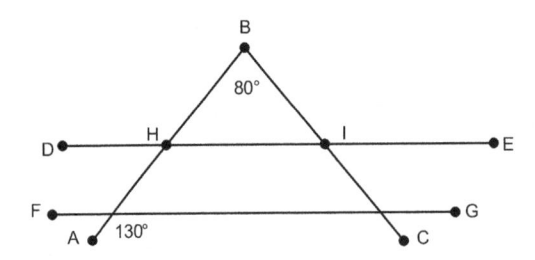

24. In the figure above, DE is parallel to FG. What is the measure of angle BIH, in degrees?

Week 13

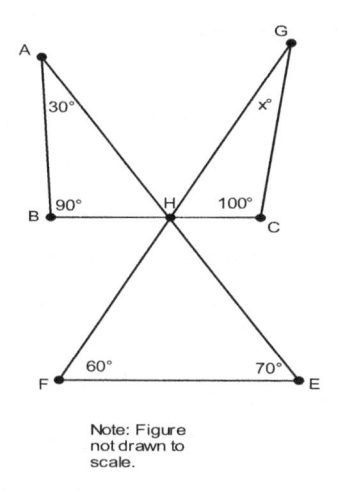

25. What is the measure of angle x, in degrees?

Questions 26 and 27 are based on the figure below, where segments AB and CD are parallel.

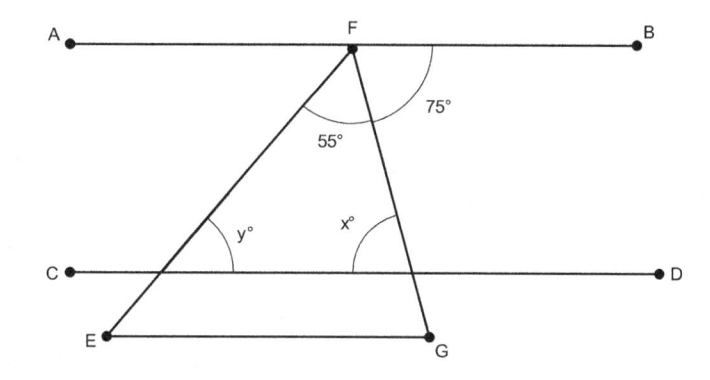

26. What is the value of x?

27. What is the value of y?

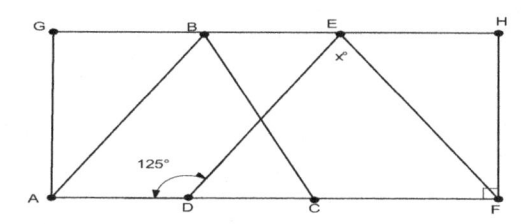

28. If $AB = BC$ and $DE = EF$, what is the value of x?

Week 13

29. Two sides of a triangle measure 3 and 22. What is a possible value of the length of the third side?

30. Two sides of a triangle measure 10 and 15. If the length of the third side is a whole number, what is the largest possible perimeter of the triangle? (Perimeter= sum of sides)

31. A triangle has sides of 10, n, and n. If n is an integer, what is the smallest possible perimeter of the triangle?

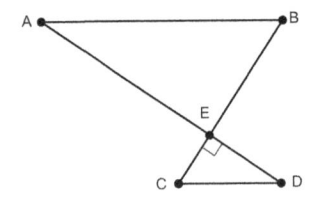

32. If angle A equals angle D and angle D measures 43 degrees, what is the measure of angle B in degrees?

Week 13

Questions 33 and 34 are based on the figure below.

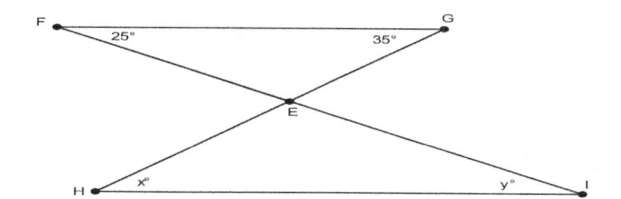

33. In the figure above triangles EFG and EIH are similar. Which of the following must be true?
   A. $\overline{FG} \parallel \overline{HI}$.
   B. $\overline{FG} \perp \overline{HI}$
   C. $\overline{HE} = \overline{EI}$
   D. $\overline{FG} = \overline{HI}$

34. What is the measure of angle x, in degrees?

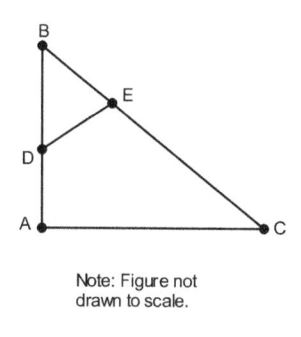

Note: Figure not drawn to scale.

35. In the figure above, angle A measures 90 degrees and DE is perpendicular to BC. If $DE = 8, BE = 2$, and $AB = 15$, what is the length of AC?

Week 13

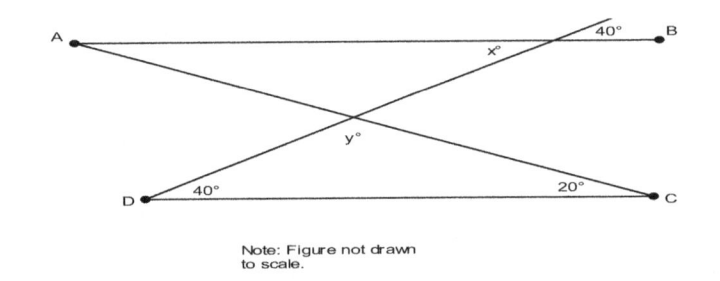

36. Which of the following must be true?
    A. Angle x is supplementary to angle y.
    B. Segment AB intersects, but is not perpendicular to, segment CD.
    C. Segment AB is parallel to segment CD.
    D. Segment AB is perpendicular to segment CD.

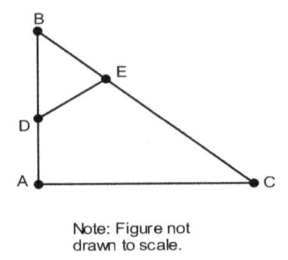

37. In the figure above, angle A measures 90 degrees and DE is perpendicular to BE. If $AB = 14$, $AC = 7$, and the length of BE is one more than the length of DE, what is the length of DE?

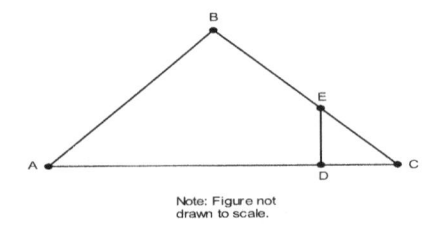

38. In the figure above, ABC and EDC are right triangles such that angles B and D are right angles. If $AB = 24$, $EC = 15$, and $ED = 12$, what is the length of AC?

Week 13

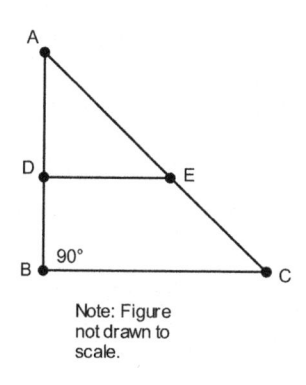

39. In the figure above, DE is parallel to BC, $AD = 12$, $DE = 3$, and AB is 10 more than BC. What is the length of BC?

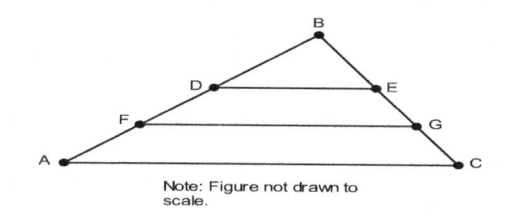

40. A book shelf shown above has three levels. $AC = 60$ inches, $FG = 40$ inches, and $DE = 20$ inches. If the shelf is 24 inches tall, how tall is the top level, in inches?

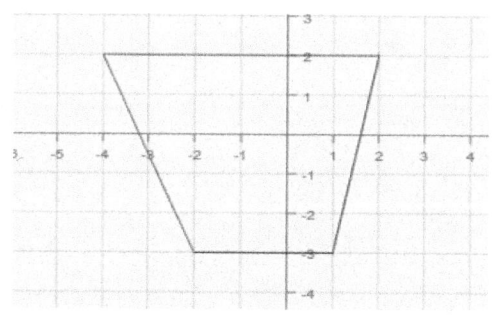

41. If the length of each box on the coordinate plane represents 4 feet, what is the area of the trapezoid above, in square feet?

Week 13

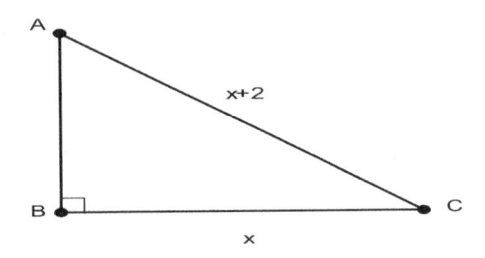

42. What is the length of AB in terms of x?

  A. $x + 1$
  B. $\sqrt{2x^2 + 4x + 4}$
  C. $\sqrt{4x + 4}$
  D. $2x + 2$

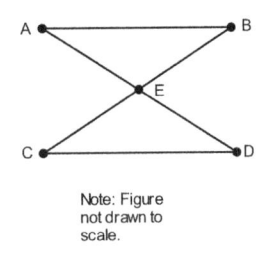

43. In the figure above, angle $AEB = 90$ degrees, angle A=angle D, $CE = 12, ED = 9$, and $BE = 20$. What is the length of AB?

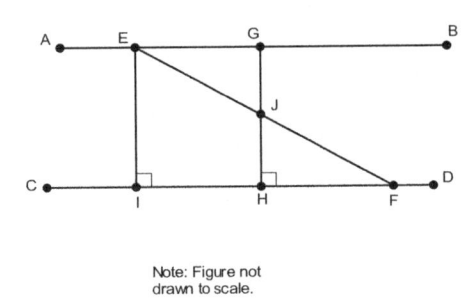

44. In the figure above, $HF = 3, EF = 17$, and $EI = 8$. What is the length of JH?

Week 13

45. An equilateral triangle has a perimeter of 18. What is the area of the triangle?
   A. $\frac{3\sqrt{3}}{2}$
   B. $3\sqrt{3}$
   C. $9\sqrt{3}$
   D. $18\sqrt{3}$

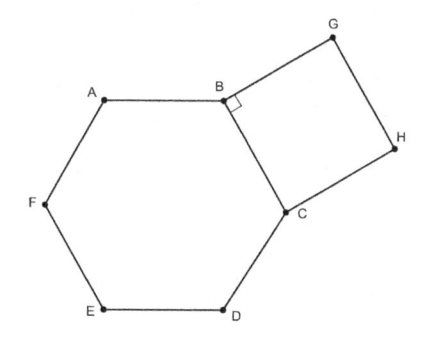

46. The area of the hexagon is $150\sqrt{3}$. What is the area of square BGHC?

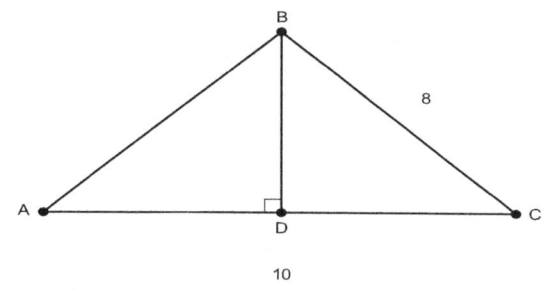

47. In the triangle above, angle A=angle C. What is the height BD?
   A. $\sqrt{3}$
   B. $\sqrt{39}$
   C. $\sqrt{89}$
   D. $\sqrt{164}$

Week 13

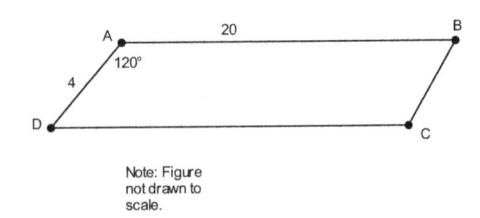

48. If $AD = 4$ and $AB = 20$, what is the area of parallelogram ABCD?

   A. 40

   B. $40\sqrt{3}$

   C. 80

   D. $80\sqrt{3}$

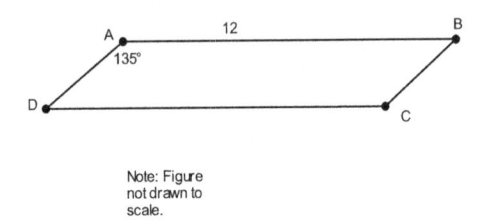

49. The area of the parallelogram above is 60. What is the value of length AD?

   A. 5

   B. $5\sqrt{2}$

   C. $5\sqrt{3}$

   D. 10

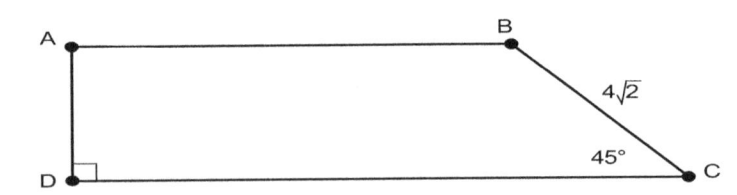

50. If the area of the quadrilateral above is 48 and $BC = 4\sqrt{2}$, what is the value of AB?

Week 13

Week 14: Circles, Solid Geometry, Trigonometry, and Complex Numbers

No Calculator

1. Which of the following is a point exterior to the circle with the equation $(x-4)^2 + y^2 = 20$?
    A. (5,1)
    B. (6,2)
    C. (7,3)
    D. (8,4)

$$(x-8)^2 + (y+2)^2 = 25$$

2. P and Q are points on a diameter of the circle with the equation above. If $P = (3, -2)$, what are the coordinates of Q?
    A. (13,-2)
    B. (8,3)
    C. (8,-7)
    D. (8,-2)

$$(x+3)^2 + (y-1)^2 = 30$$

3. What is the area of the circle with the equation above?
    A. 15π
    B. 225π
    C. 30π
    D. 900π

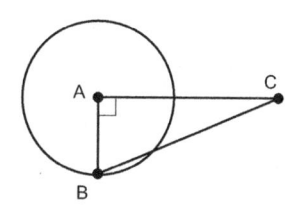

4. In the figure above, AB is the radius of circle A, $AC = 1.2$, and $BC = 1.3$. What is the diameter of the circle?

Week 14

$$x^2 + 8x + y^2 + 2y = 10$$

5. What is the radius of the circle with the equation above?

    A. $\sqrt{10}$

    B. $\sqrt{20}$

    C. $\sqrt{27}$

    D. $\sqrt{35}$

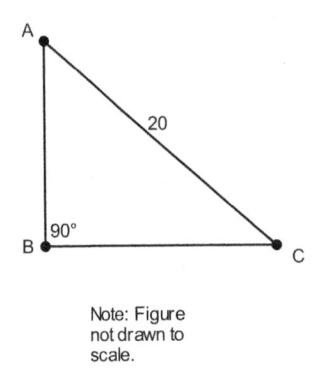

Note: Figure not drawn to scale.

6. In the figure above, if tan C = $\frac{4}{3}$, what is length of BC?

7. Triangles ABC and DEF are similar such that vertices A and D, B and E, and C and F correspond. Each side of DEF is one fourth that of ABC. Angle B and angle E are right angles. $AB = 15$, and $BC = 20$. What is sine D?

Week 14

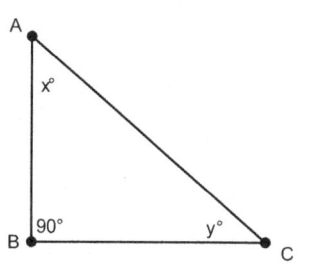

8. In the figure above, what is the value of $\cos x - \sin y$?

9. A container is in the shape of a right circular cylinder. The base of the cylinder has an area of 40 cubic centimeters and the height of the cylinder is 10 centimeters. The volume of a figurine in the container is 90 cubic centimeters. If the rest of the container is entirely filled with foam, which of the following is closest to the volume of the foam?
   A. 50 cubic centimeters
   B. 140 cubic centimeters
   C. 310 cubic centimeters
   D. 400 cubic centimeters

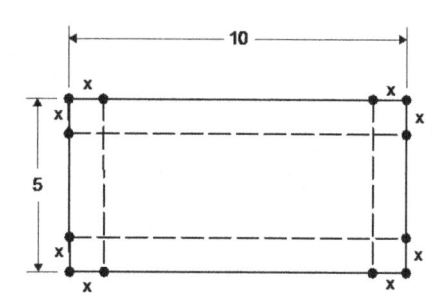

10. A piece of rectangular cardboard shown above measures 10 inches by 5 inches. Four squares on each corner with a perimeter of $4x$ inches will be cut from the cardboard, and the carboard will then be folded into a rectangular box with an open top. Which of the following expressions for the volume of the box includes an expression representing the area of the base of the box?
    A. $(4x^2 - 30x + 50)(x)$
    B. $4x^3 - 30x^2 + 50x$
    C. $(2x^2 - 5x)(2x - 10)$
    D. $(4x - 10)(x - 5)$

Week 14

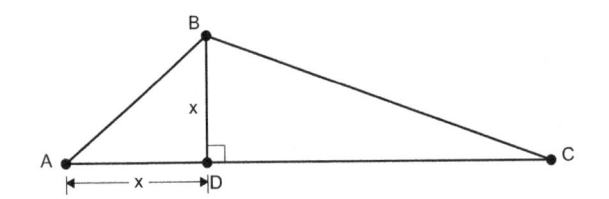

11. In the figure above, the area of triangle ABC is $5x^2$. What is the sine of $\angle C$?

A. $\dfrac{1}{\sqrt{82}}$

B. $\sqrt{82}$

C. $\dfrac{1}{9}$

D. 9

12. In the xy-plane, which of the following is true of the circle with the equation $(x-4)^2 + (y-2)^2 = .25$ and the line $.5x = y$?
   A. The line is tangent to the circle at one point
   B. The line divides the circle into two congruent arcs
   C. The line divides the circle into two unequal arcs
   D. The line and the circle never intersect

13. In triangle DEF with right angle E, $\cos D = \dfrac{5}{13}$. What is tan F?

A. $\dfrac{5}{12}$

B. $\dfrac{5}{13}$

C. $\dfrac{12}{5}$

D. $\dfrac{13}{5}$

14. If $(12 + 2i)(3 - 4i) = a + bi$, what is the value of a? ($i = \sqrt{-1}$)

Week 14

Calculator

$$S = 2Cr$$

15. The formula above relates the approximate surface area of a planet, S, to its average circumference, C, and average radius, r. If the surface area of a planet is 5.9×10^9 square miles, which of the following best approximates its radius, in miles?
    A. 2.2×10^4
    B. 3.1×10^4
    C. 9.6×10^6
    D. 9.4×10^8

Questions 16 and 17 are based on the information below.

In one revolution, a car travels a distance equivalent to the circumference of one of its tires.

16. A certain car does 800 revolutions per minute and its tires have a radius of .2 meters. To the nearest integer, what is the car's speed in kilometers per hour?

17. A certain toy car travels 320π inches in one minute, which is equivalent to 40 revolutions. What is the radius of one of its tires, in inches? (Assume all tires have the same radius.)

18. Which of the following equations represents a circle with radius 6 that passes through the origin?
    A. $(x - 3)^2 + (y + 3)^2 = 6$
    B. $(x - 3)^2 + (y + 3)^2 = 36$
    C. $(x - 2\sqrt{3})^2 + (y + 2\sqrt{3})^2 = 36$
    D. $(x - 3\sqrt{2})^2 + (y + 3\sqrt{2})^2 = 36$

Week 14

Questions 19 to 21 are based on the situation below.

$$a = 7.5d$$

The age of a Shagbark Hickory tree can be modeled by the equation above, where a is its age in years and d is its diameter in inches.

19. A certain tree has an area of 144π square inches. According to the model, how old is the tree, in years?

20. If a certain Shagbark Hickory is 120 years old, what is the approximate circumference of the tree, in feet? (12 inches= 1 foot)
    A. $\frac{3}{4}\pi$
    B. $\frac{4}{3}\pi$
    C. 8π
    D. 16π

21. One Shagbark Hickory has a diameter of 2 feet. What will be its area in 15 years, in square inches? (Round to the nearest integer).

22. A circle has the equation $2x^2 + 10x + 2y^2 - 2y = 19$. What is the diameter of the circle?
    A. 2
    B. 4
    C. 8
    D. 16

$$x^2 + 6x + y^2 + 4y = 2$$

23. What is the center of the circle with the equation above?
    A. (-3,-2)
    B. (3,2)
    C. (-4,-6)

Week 14

D. (4,6)

24. Cups in the shape of a right circular cylinder have a diameter of 5 inches and a height of 4 inches. Water is poured from a one-gallon jug into glasses until no water remains. What is the largest number of full glasses of water that can be poured? (1 gallon=231 cubic inches)
   A. 2
   B. 3
   C. 4
   D. 5

25. Angle x and angle y are acute angles such that $sinx = cosy$. If $x = 2k + 10$ and $y = 3k + 5$, what is the value of k?

26. A right circular cylinder has a height of 10 centimeters and a volume of 800 cubic centimeters. A second right cylinder has a base with the same area but a volume of 560 cubic centimeters. What is the height of the second right cylinder, in centimeters?

27. A tank has a length of 40 centimeters, a width of 30 centimeters, and a height of 60 centimeters. The depth of the water in the tank before a toy is added is 30 centimeters. After the toy is added, the new depth is 30.6 centimeters. What is the volume of the toy, in cubic centimeters?

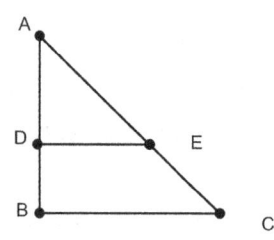

28. In the figure above (not drawn to scale) $cos A = \frac{3}{5}$, $BC = 20$ and $DB = 6$, what is the length of AE?

Week 14

29. If $\frac{3+i}{2-i} = a + bi$, what is the value of a?

30. What is the value of $\frac{i^4 - 9}{i^2 - 3}$?

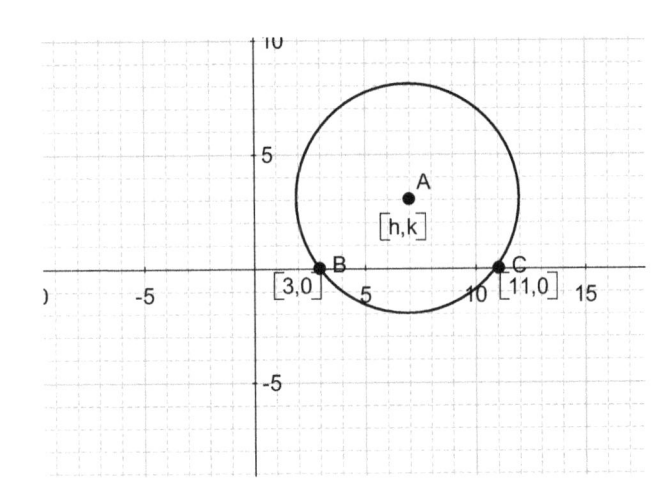

31. The circle with the center (h, k) shown above has a radius of 5. What is the value of k?

32. A circle has a diameter with the endpoints (-2,-4) and (8,4). If $(0, p)$ is a point on the circle and $p > 0$, what is the value of p?
   A. $\sqrt{32}$
   B. $\sqrt{41}$
   C. $\sqrt{235}$
   D. $\sqrt{244}$

Week 14

33. What is the equation of the circle with (3,2) and (-3,-2) as endpoints of one of its diameters?
   A. $(x-3)^2 + (y+2)^2 = 13$
   B. $(x+3)^2 + (y-2)^2 = 52$
   C. $x^2 + y^2 = 13$
   D. $x^2 + y^2 = 52$

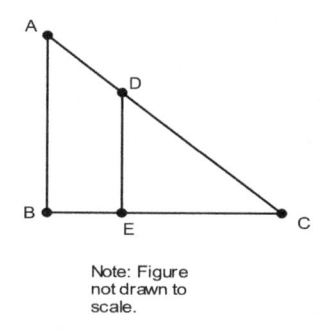

Note: Figure not drawn to scale.

34. In the figure above, angle B= 90 degrees, angle E= 90 degrees, AB is parallel to DE, and $\tan A = 1.5$. If $EC = 60$, what is the length of DE?

35. The area of a sector of a circle with central angle A measuring x degrees is between 10 and 11 square inches. If the radius of the circle is 4 inches, what is a possible integer value of x? (Use 3.14 for π.)

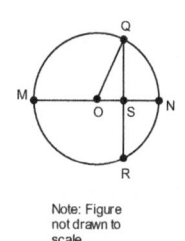

Note: Figure not drawn to scale.

36. In the figure above of the circle with center O, diameter MN is perpendicular to chord QR. If $QR = 80$, and $NS = 20$, what is the length of OQ?

Week 14

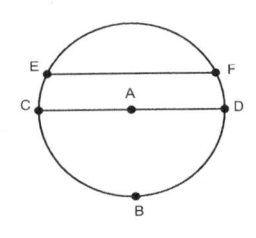

Note: Figure not drawn to scale.

37. In the figure above, chord EF is parallel to the diameter of the circle with center A. If the length of EF is half the length of the diameter of the circle, what is the distance between the chord and the center of the circle in terms of the circle's radius, r?

   A. r^2

   B. $\sqrt{r}$

   C. $\sqrt{\frac{1}{2}}r$

   D. $\frac{\sqrt{3}}{2}r$

Questions 38 and 39 are based on the figure below. MQ is tangent to the radius OM, which equals 4.

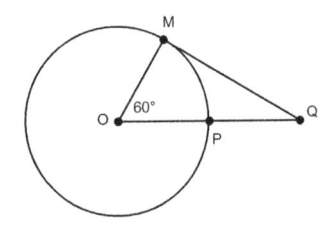

38. What is the length of OQ?

39. How much greater is the area of OMQ than the area of sector MOP?

   A. $16\sqrt{3} - \frac{8}{3}\pi$

   B. $16\sqrt{3} - \frac{16}{3}\pi$

   C. $8\sqrt{3} - \frac{8}{3}\pi$

   D. $8\sqrt{3} - \frac{16}{3}\pi$

Week 14

Questions 40 and 41 are based on the figure below.

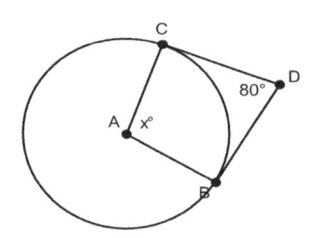

In the figure above, segments CD and BD are tangent to the circle.

40. What is the value of x?

41. If the circumference of the circle is 18, what is the length of minor arc BC?

42. Which of the following is the equation of a circle with a center of (0,2) and the diameter with endpoint of $(\frac{4}{3}, 3)$?

A. $x^2 + (y+2)^2 = \frac{25}{9}$
B. $x^2 + (y-2)^2 = \frac{5}{3}$
C. $x^2 + (y+2)^2 = \frac{5}{3}$
D. $x^2 + (y-2)^2 = \frac{25}{9}$

43. A circle has a diameter with endpoints (1,6) and (3,12). What is the equation of the circle?

A. $(x-2)^2 + (y-9)^2 = 10$
B. $(x-2)^2 + (y-9)^2 = 40$
C. $(x-4)^2 + (y-18)^2 = 10$
D. $(x-4)^2 + (y-18)^2 = 40$

Week 14

Note: Figure not drawn to scale.

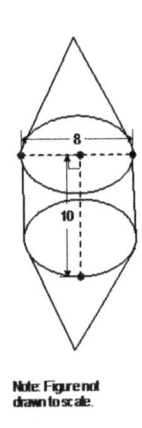

44. The silo consists of a right circular cylinder and two identical cones with a common base. The height of each cone is 6 inches. Which of the following is closest to the volume of the silo, in cubic inches?

    A. 224
    B. 704
    C. 896
    D. 2,815

45. The area of the base of a rectangular prism is 42 cubic centimeters. The length is 4 centimeters more than the height and the width is 7 centimeters less than the height. What is the volume of the prism, in cubic centimeters?

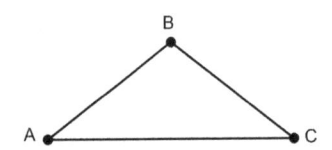

46. In the figure above, $AB = BC = 20$, and $AC = 32$. What is the value of the sine of angle A?

Week 14

47. Angles R and U are right angles of similar triangles QRS and TUV such that each side of TUV is $\frac{1}{4}$ as big as the corresponding sides of QRS. Vertices Q,R, and S correspond to vertices T,U, and V respectively. Side $QR = 20$ and side $RS = 48$. What is the value of sin T?

   A. $\frac{4}{13}$
   B. $\frac{5}{13}$
   C. $\frac{10}{13}$
   D. $\frac{12}{13}$

48. If $sin(6a + 12) = cos(2a + 14)$ and a is measured in degrees, what is the value of the smaller angle when $0 < a < 90$?

49. The cosine of an angle measuring $\frac{\pi}{4}$ radians is equal to the measure of the sine of an angle measuring how many radians?

   A. 0
   B. $\frac{\pi}{8}$
   C. $\frac{\pi}{4}$
   D. $\frac{3\pi}{4}$

50. If $\pi < x < \frac{3\pi}{2}$, $sinx = w$, and $sin\ y = -w$, which of the following could be the value of y?

   A. $x + 4\pi$
   B. $x - 8\pi$
   C. $6\pi - x$
   D. $3\pi - x$

Week 14

Key

Week 1

1. **B.** When $|x-2|-2=0$, and $|x-2|=2$. Thus, $x-2=2$ and $x=4$ or $x-2=-2$, and $x=0$. The other choices will always be greater than or equal to 2 (whatever is inside the absolute value sign is at least 0 and 2 is added to the final answer).
2. **1.5 or $\frac{3}{2}$.** $2.4(h+2) = .3h + 7.95, 2.4h + 4.8 = .3h + 7.95, 2.1h = 3.15, 210h = 315$, and $h = 1.5$.
3. **.7 or $\frac{7}{10}$.** $-2k + 4 = -2k + 4k + 1.2, 2.8 = 4k$, and $.7 = k$.
4. **10.** $705 = \frac{7(5(50)-4c)}{2} - 30, 735 = \frac{7(250-4c)}{2}, 1470 = 7(250-4c), 210 = 250 - 4c, 4c = 40$, and $c = 10$.
5. **11.** The slope of line k is $\frac{17-7}{6-1} = \frac{10}{5} = 2$. The parallel line m has the same slope. $\frac{n-5}{4-1} = 2, \frac{n-5}{3} = 2$, $n - 5 = 6$, and $n = 11$.
6. **D.** The line has an equation of $y = \frac{1}{9}x$. (27,3) satisfies this equation since $3 = \frac{1}{9}(27)$, and $3 = 3$.
7. **11.** $\frac{5x-15}{2} = \frac{10x-50}{3}$, $2(10x - 50) = 3(5x - 15), 20x - 100 = 15x - 45, 5x = 55$, and $x = 11$.
8. **D.** The distance between x and -2 is $|x - (-2)| = |x + 2|$. This difference equals 5. You can also determine that -7 is 5 units left of -2 on the number line and 3 is 5 units right. Only D satisfies both solutions.
9. **B.** If a line has a positive slope, it passes through Quadrants I and III. If it has a negative y-intercept, it passes through III and IV. Thus, it does not pass through Quadrant II, which includes (-2,5).
10. **A.** $-6ay = -ax + 1, y = \frac{-ax}{-6a} + \frac{1}{-6a}$, and $y = \frac{1}{6}x + \frac{-1}{6a}$. The slope is $\frac{1}{6}$.
11. **1.** If $k + n = 0$, then k and n are additive inverses. Thus, $k = -n$ since $-n + n = 0$. The slope is $\frac{n-(k)}{-k-(-n)} = \frac{n-k}{-k+n} = \frac{n-(-n)}{-(-n)+n} = \frac{n+n}{n+n} = \frac{2n}{2n} = 1$.
12. **18.** The slope of k is $\frac{4-3}{10-8} = \frac{1}{2}$. The slope of line m is -2. $\frac{10-c}{5-1} = \frac{-2}{1}, 10 - c = -8$, and $18 = c$.
13. **2.5 or $\frac{5}{2}$.** Plug in 0 for y. $6x + 7(0) = 15, 6x = 15, x = \frac{15}{6}$, and $x = \frac{5}{2}$.
14. **4.8 or $\frac{24}{5}$.** First find the slope of the line. It contains the point (5,5) and (0,-7). $\frac{5-(-7)}{5-0} = \frac{12}{5}$. Thus, the equation of the parallel line is $y = \frac{12}{5}x + b$, where b is the y-intercept. Since (-2,0) is a point on the line, plug in the coordinates and solve for b. $0 = \frac{12}{5}(-2) + b, 0 = \frac{-24}{5} + b$, and $\frac{24}{5} = b$.
15. **A.** Rearrange the first equation to get $x = 8y$. Substitute $8y$ for x in the second equation. $2(y + 3) = 8y - 6, 2y + 6 = 8y - 6, 12 = 6y$, and $2 = y$.
16. **C.** $\frac{5}{2}a + 4 = \frac{1}{2}(5a + 4), \frac{5}{2}a + 4 = \frac{5}{2}a + 2$, and $2 = 0$, which is not a true statement. Thus, there are no solutions.
17. **241.** The easiest way to solve without a calculator is to multiply both sides by 100 to yield $8(250 - x) = 72$. Then divide both sides by 8 to yield $250 - x = 9$, and $x = 241$.
18. **5.** $4|-2x + 8| + 2 = 10, 4|-2x + 8| = 8$, and $|-2x + 8| = 2$. Thus, $-2x + 8 = 2$ or $-2x + 8 = -2$. If $-2x + 8 = -2, -2x = -10$, and $x = 5$.
19. **.6 or $\frac{3}{5}$.** Plug in 0 for y. $\frac{5}{3}x + 2(0) = 1, \frac{5}{3}x = 1$, and $x = \frac{3}{5}$.

20. **B.** Divide both sides by 2 to yield $x + y = \frac{5}{2}$.
21. **2.** $2a + 4b = 6\left(\frac{1}{3}a + \frac{2}{3}b\right)$, $12 = 6\left(\frac{1}{3}a + \frac{2}{3}b\right)$, and $2 = \left(\frac{1}{3}a + \frac{2}{3}b\right)$.
22. **190.** If $\frac{1}{2}(3x + 8y) = 20$, then $3x + 8y = 40$. Since $15x + 40y = 5(3x + 8y)$, then $15x + 40y = 5(40) = 200$. Thus, $15x + 40y - 10 = 200 - 10 = 190$.
23. **C.** The slope of the line is $\frac{3-0}{k-0} = \frac{3}{k}$. The slope of the line is also $\frac{k-0}{4-0} = \frac{k}{4}$. Thus, $\frac{k}{4} = \frac{3}{k}$, $k^2 = 12$, and $k = \sqrt{12}$.
24. **10.** Multiply the top equation by -12 to yield $-18x - 4y = -48$. Add the two equations to yield $-17x = -68$, and $x = 4$. If $x = 4$, then $4 + 4y = -20, 4y = -24$, and $y = -6$. Thus, $x - y = 4 - (-6) = 10$.
25. **14.** $20a + 20b = 4(5a + 5b)$. Since $20a + 20b = 48$, $48 = 4(5a + 5b)$, and $12 = 5a + 5b$. Thus, $5a + 5b + 2 = 12 + 2 = 14$.
26. **B.** You can rewrite the top equation with a denominator of 8. $\frac{4}{8}x + \frac{2}{8}y = 2$. Multiply the bottom equation by -2 to yield $-\frac{2}{8}x - \frac{2}{8}y = -16$. Add the equations to yield $\frac{2}{8}x = -14, \frac{1}{4}x = -14$, and $x = -56$. If $x = -56, \frac{1}{2}(-56) + \frac{1}{4}y = 2, -28 + \frac{1}{4}y = 2, \frac{1}{4}y = 30$, and $y = 120$.
27. **7.** If $x = \frac{1}{4}y$, then $4x = y$. Substitute $4x$ for y in the second equation. $182 - 3(4x) = 14x, 182 = 26x$, and $7 = x$.
28. **.4 or $\frac{2}{5}$.** One equation must be an exact multiple of the other for the equation to have an infinite number of solutions. Let $n =$ the constant of multiplication. $20n = 100$, so $n = 5$. Thus, the second equation is 5 times the first. $5a = 8$, and $a = \frac{8}{5}$. $5b = 6$, and $b = \frac{6}{5}$. $a - b = \frac{8}{5} - \frac{6}{5} = \frac{2}{5}$.
29. **$\frac{4}{7}$.** One equation must be an exact multiple of the other for the equation to have an infinite number of solutions. Let $n =$ the constant of multiplication. $12n = 36$, and $n = 3$. Thus, $3a = 4$, and $a = \frac{4}{3}$ and $3b = 7$, and $b = \frac{7}{3}$. $\frac{a}{b} = \frac{4}{3} \div \frac{7}{3} = \frac{4}{7}$.
30. **1.2 or $\frac{6}{5}$.** If a system of equations has no solution, then only the coefficients of the x and y terms are multiplied by the same constant (the lines are parallel and have equal slopes but different y-intercepts). Let the constant of multiplication$= n$. $4n = 20$, and $n = 5$. Thus, $5a = 6$, and $a = \frac{6}{5}$.
31. **4.2 or $\frac{21}{5}$.** If a system of equations has no solution, then only the coefficients of the x and y terms are multiplied by the same constant (the lines are parallel and have equal slopes but different y-intercepts). Let the constant of multiplication$= n$. $7n = 5$, and $n = \frac{5}{7}$. Thus, $\frac{5}{7}a = 3$, and $a = \frac{21}{5}$.
32. **5.33 or $\frac{16}{3}$.** If a system of equations has no solution, then only the coefficients of the x and y terms are multiplied by the same constant (the lines are parallel and have equal slopes but different y-intercepts). Let the constant of multiplication$= n$. $3n = 8$, and $n = \frac{8}{3}$. Thus, $a = 2(\frac{8}{3}) = \frac{16}{3}$.
33. **B.** $a + 1 = 3b + 5c$, so $a = 3b + 5c - 1$. Thus, $2b + 4c = 3b + 5c - 1$, and $-c + 1 = b$.
34. **C.** $3x = 4y + 2z + 1$. Thus, $4y + 2z + 1 = 8y - 4z, 6z = 4y - 1, z = \frac{4}{6}y - \frac{1}{6}$, and $z = \frac{2}{3}y - \frac{1}{6}$.
35. **D.** The line $y = 5$ is a horizontal line with a slope of 0. A perpendicular line would have an undefined slope and take the form $x = c$, where c is a constant.

127

36. **4.** The slope is 3 and the y-intercept is n, so $y = 3x + n$. Since $n = p + 8$, $y = 3x + (p + 8)$. If $(p, 0)$ is a coordinate on the line, $0 = 3p + (p + 8)$, $0 = 4p + 8$, $-8 = 4p$, and $-2 = p$. Thus, $n = -2 + 8 = 6$. Thus, $p + n = -2 + 6 = 4$.

37. **4.** First find the slope of f using any two coordinates such as $(0,2)$ and $(1,-2)$. $\frac{-2-2}{1-0} = \frac{-4}{1} = -4$. The perpendicular line g has a slope of $\frac{1}{4}$. Thus, $g(x) = \frac{1}{4}x + b$, where b is the y-intercept, or $g(0)$. Since $(4,5)$ is a solution $5 = \frac{1}{4}(4) + b$, $5 = 1 + b$, and $4 = b$. Thus, $g(0) = 4$.

38. **D.** The slope of AB is $\frac{3-0}{2-0} = \frac{3}{2}$. Thus, the slope of BC is $-\frac{2}{3}$. $\frac{3-0}{2-p} = \frac{-2}{3}$, $9 = -2(2-p)$, $9 = -4 + 2p$, $13 = 2p$, and $6.5 = p$.

Week 2

1. **A.** The change in miles walked per week is the slope (change in miles divided by change in time). $\frac{16-10}{8-4} = \frac{6}{4} = 1.5$.
2. **B.** The slope is -3, so as the temperature increases by 1 degree, the number of customers decreases by 3. Thus, as the temperature decreases by 1 degree, the number of customers increases by 3.
3. **.5 or $\frac{1}{2}$.** $y = \frac{x+5}{2}$ can be rewritten as $y = \frac{1}{2}(x+5) = \frac{1}{2}x + 2.5$. The slope is $\frac{1}{2}$ so as x increases by 1, y increases by $\frac{1}{2}$. You can also pick numbers. For example, when $x = 1, y = 3$. When x increases by 1 to become 2, $y = 3.5$.
4. **D.** The slope is $\frac{4}{3}$ so as c increases by 1, d increases by $\frac{4}{3}$. As d increases by 1, c increases by the reciprocal, which is $\frac{3}{4}$, or .75.
5. **B.** The slope is $-\frac{1}{400}$ which means that the height decreases by $\frac{1}{400}$ of a foot each year. In 100 years, the change is $100 \times -\frac{1}{400} = -\frac{1}{4}$.
6. **C.** Since the equation is in thousands, the actual slope is $-50 \times 1{,}000 = -50{,}000$. Thus, the population decreases by 50,000 each year.
7. **B.** The slope is 2. As the number of pails increases by 1, the height increases by 2 inches.
8. **.5 or $\frac{1}{2}$.** The slope is 2 so as perimeter increases by 1 foot, area increases by 2 square feet. Thus, as area increases by 1 square foot, perimeter increases by the reciprocal ($\frac{1}{2}$ foot).
9. **D.** The y-intercept is the value of y when $x = 0$. In context, it is the height of the candle when it is first burned.
10. **B.** The number of cows is equivalent to the number of number of horses multiplied by 3.
11. **A.** The starting temperature at sea level (the y-intercept) is 30. Since the temperature decreases by 1 degree per 20 feet, it decreases by $\frac{1}{20}$ of a degree per foot (the slope). Thus, $C = 30 - \frac{1}{20}f$, and $C = 30 - \frac{f}{20}$.
12. **C.** Let the height of the shorter roller coaster$= x$ and the height of the taller roller coaster$= x + 36$. Thus, $x + x + 36 = 876, 2x + 36 = 876, 2x = 840$, and $x = 420$. Thus, the large roller coaster has a height of $420 + 36 = 456$.
13. **58.** There are $60 + 27 = 87$ minutes in 1 hour and 27 minutes. Let the amount of time on Tuesday$= x$ and the amount of Wednesday$= 2x$. Thus, $2x + x = 87, 3x = 87$, and $x = 29$. On Wednesday, she studied $2(29) = 58$ minutes.
14. **B.** The slope is $\frac{\frac{11}{3}-\frac{7}{3}}{2-1} = \frac{4}{3}$. Thus, $y = \frac{4}{3}x + b$ where b is the y-intercept. To determine the y-intercept, plug in a set of coordinates. $\frac{7}{3} = \frac{4}{3}(1) + b$, and $1 = b$.
15. **D.** The number of birds is double the number of lizards, so $2l = b$.
16. **D.** If the number of customers decreases by 900 per 10 degrees, it decreases by $\frac{900}{10} = 90$ customers per one degree. The slope is -90 and the y-intercept is 562 since there are 562 customers at 0 degrees. Thus, $f(t) = 562 - 90t$.
17. **B.** The slope is $\frac{100-24}{19} = 4$. The y-intercept is 24 (the original temperature). Thus, $T = 24 + 4s$.

18. **D.** The cost of the first 400 books is $400 \times 10 = \$4000$. The remaining $x - 400$ books costs $8 each, so the cost for those is $\$8(x - 400)$. For example, if there are 500 books, $500 - 400 = 100$ books are sold at the $8 rate. Thus, $C = 4000 + 8(x - 400)$.

19. **B.** If the boiling point drops .1 degree per 100 feet, it drops $.1 \div 100 = .001$ degrees per foot. The slope is $-.001$ and the y-intercept (the boiling point at 0 feet above sea level) is 100. Thus, $B = 100 - .001t$.

20. **A.** The y-intercept is 2.8 (the original budget). The slope is $\frac{2.8-1.1}{1992-2003} = -\frac{1.7}{11} = -\frac{17}{100}$. Thus, $f(t) = 2.8 - \frac{17}{100}t$.

21. **8.** The change in degrees per kilometer is $\frac{-5-(-25)}{50-75} = \frac{20}{-25} = -\frac{4}{5}$. Thus, the change per 10 kilometers is $-\frac{4}{5} \times 10 = -8$. Thus, the temperature decreases by 8 degrees per 10 kilometers.

22. **D.** Each month it gains 2,000 and loses 500 subscribers, for a net gain of $2,000 - 500 = 1,500$ subscribers. Thus, the slope is 1500 and the y-intercept (the original number of subscribers) is 1800. $s = 1800 + 1500m$.

23. **A.** Profit is revenue minus expenses. If she spends $8 to make each figure and sells them for $25, her profit is $\$25 - \$8 = \$17$. Thus, $P = 17x$.

24. **B.** 565 is the y-intercept, the value of distance when time= 0. In this case, that is the distance the train must travel between the cities.

25. **A.** -120 is the slope, or the number of miles traveled per hour (the speed).

26. **4.7.** When the distance between the cities is 0, the train has traveled from one city to the next. $0 = 565 - 120t$, $120t = 565$, and $t \approx 4.7$.

27. **B.** a is the slope, the change in height per day.

28. **B.** Find the slope (change in height per day) between days 7 and 14. $\frac{2.67-2.16}{14-7} \approx .072$. Thus, $h = .072t + b$, where b is the y-intercept. Plug in coordinates to find b. $7 = .072(2.16) + b$, and $1.66 = b$.

29. **C.** Use any two points from the table to find the slope. $\frac{8,000,000-5,900,000}{8100-6000} = 1000$. Thus, $R = 1000x + b$, where b is the y-intercept. Test a set of values on the table to find the y-intercept. $8,000,000 = 1000(8100) + b$, and $-100,000 = b$.

30. **A.** Since we are asked to put price in thousands of dollars, divide each price by 1,000. For example, 120,000 dollars= 120 thousand dollars. The table is reproduced below to account for the change.

Mortgage (in dollars)	Price (in thousands of dollars)
1,000	120
1,510	180
1,935	230
2,955	350
4,570	540

Find the slope: In this case, mortgage is y and price is x since we are asked to find mortgage as a function of price. Pick any two rows on the table to find the slope: $\frac{1510-1000}{180-120} = 8.5$. Thus, $m(p) = 8.5p + b$ where b is the y-intercept. Test a point on the table to find b. $1,000 = 8.5(120) + b$, $1,000 = 1,020 + b$, and $-20 = b$.

31. **85.** Let the cost of each hat= h and the cost of each umbrella= $h + 20$. Thus, the costs of 2 hats and 3 umbrellas is $2h + 3(h + 20) = 2h + 3h + 60 = 5h + 60$. Thus, $385 = 5h + 60, 325 = 5h$, and $65 = h$. Thus, the umbrella costs $65 + 20 = \$85$.
32. **22.** Let the integers, in order from smallest to largest, equal $x, x + 2, x + 4, x + 6$, and $x + 8$. Thus, $x + x + 4 = x + 8 + 16, 2x + 4 = x + 24$, and $x = 20$. Thus, the second integer is $x + 2 = 20 + 2 = 22$.
33. **B.** The y-intercept is 905 (the starting population). The slope is $\frac{950-905}{2010-2005} = 9$. Thus, $P = 905 + 9t$.
34. **C.** The number of people is 4 more than 6 times the number of tables for each point on the table. Thus, $6n + 4$ is correct.
35. **D.** The times decrease for both students since the slopes are negative. It decreases faster for Student 2 since the absolute value of the slope is greater.
36. **C.** The hourly rate after 5:00 p.m. is $22.40 ($2.40 more than $20). $22.40h$ dollars are earned for work after 5:00. For the remaining $50 - h$ hours, $20(50 - h)$ dollars are earned. Thus, $f(h) = 20(50 - h) + 22.40h$.
37. **C.** The x-intercept is the time at which the number of gadgets remaining to be repaired equals 0, which is about $\frac{120}{16} = 7.5$ hours (16 are fixed per hour and there are 120 gadgets total to be fixed).
38. **7.** The slope is $\frac{3-(-7)}{3-(-2)} = \frac{10}{5} = 2$. $h(x) = 2x + b$, such that b is the y-intercept. Plug in a set of coordinates to find b. $-15 = 2(-6) + b, -15 = -12 + b$, and $-3 = b$. Thus, $h(x) = 2x - 3$, and $h(5) = 2(5) - 3 = 10 - 3 = 7$.
39. **B.** For each row after the first another 4 seats are added to 20. Since the 40th row is 39 rows after the first, there are $20 + 4(39)$ seats.

Row	Seats
1	20
2	$20 + 4 = 24$
3	$20 + 4(2) = 28$
4	$20 + 4(3) = 32$

Week 3

1. **39.** Let $x =$ the number of 4-student teams and $y =$ the number of 3-student teams. $x + y = 60$ and $4x + 3y = 219$. Multiply the first equation by -3 to yield $-3x - 3y = -180$. Add the equations to yield $x = 39$.
2. **25.** Let $b =$ the number of bracelets sold and $n =$ the number of necklaces sold. Thus, $40b + 60n = 3700$ and $b + n = 80$. Multiply the second equation by -40 to yield $-40b - 40n = -3200$. Add the equations together to yield $20n = 500$, and $n = 25$.
3. **27.** Let the number of luxury suites$= x$ and the number of standard suites$= y$. Thus, $x + y = 100$ and $100x + 60y = 7080$. To solve for x, multiply the first equation by -60 to yield $-60x - 60y = -6000$. Add the equations to yield $40x = 1080$, and $x = 27$.
4. **C.** If he sells each dozen for $6 and it costs him $2 to bake each dozen, his net profit is $4 per dozen sold. To recoup the fee for selling x dozens, $4x > 81$, and $x > 20.25$. Thus, 21 must be sold.
5. **10.** Let the number of packs of black cartridges sold$= x$ and the number of color cartridge packs$= x + 3$. Thus, $30x + 40(x + 3) = 820, 30x + 40x + 120 = 820, 70x = 700$, and $x = 10$.
6. **B.** The total number of workers must be at minimum (greater than or equal to) 10. Thus, $x + y \geq 10$. The salaries can be no more than the budget (less than or equal to) 14500. Thus, $800x + 1200y \leq 14500$. The number of analysts must be greater than or equal to 4 (at least 4) and the number of associates must be greater than or equal to 2 (at least 2).
7. **C.** The smallest possible length of all 16 pieces is $140 \times 16 = 2240$. The largest possible length is $150 \times 16 = 2400$. Thus, $2240 \leq x \leq 2400$.
8. **C.** The cost is $5f + 8p$, which must be greater than or equal to 40. Since there is at least one plate and at least one fork, p and f are each greater than or equal to 1.
9. **A.** The cost per red block is $4.50 and the cost per white block is $5.35 so the cost for all blocks is $4.50r + 5.35w$, which is greater than or equal to 100 (at least 100). Since there are twice as many red blocks as white blocks, the number of red blocks is double the number of white blocks, so $r = 2w$.
10. **C.** The cost is $2.50m + 5.60p$, which must be less than or equal to 120 (the maximum the teacher can spend). If both magazines and books are bought, each of these values must be greater than or equal to 1.
11. **B.** Let the number of sofas$= x$. $75x + 35(30) + 300 \leq 2,000, 75x \leq 650, x < 8.66$, so 8 is the maximum.
12. **D.** Add 7 to both sides of the bottom inequality to yield $2x + 7 > 2 + 7$, or $2x + 7 > 9$. If $y > 2x + 7$ and $2x + 7 > 9$, then $y > 9$ by the transitive property of inequality.
13. **D.** The total number of tickets $(x + y)$ is less than or equal to the maximum number of tickets (2,000). The profit, $5x + 8y$, must be greater than $12,000.
14. **D.** Ira's total travel time when taking the bus is $x + 6$ (x minutes for waiting and 6 minutes for travel). In order for walking to be faster, this time must be greater than 18 minutes.
15. **C.** If x artists presented 2 works each, $2x$ were submitted by these artists. The remaining $10 - x$ submitted 3 works each, so $3(10 - x) = 30 - 3x$. The total number of submissions was $2x + 30 - 3x = -x + 30$.

132

16. **C.** $185 = a(20)^2 - c$, so $185 = 400a - c$ and $17 = a(8)^2 - c$, so $17 = 64a - c$. We now have a system of equations. Multiply the second equation by -1 to yield $-17 = -64a + c$ and add this to the first equation to yield $168 = 336a$, so $.5 = a$. If $.5 = a$, plug in $.5$ for a into either equation to find c. $185 = 400(.5) - c$, $185 = 200 - c$, and $c = 15$.

17. **B.** The cost savings per month is $3070 - 2512$, so the cost savings after x months is $(3,070 - 2,512)x$. This savings must be greater than 10,000.

18. **20.** Let $x =$ the number of correct answers and $y =$ the number of incorrect answers. Thus, $x + y = 30$ and $4x - y = 70$. Add the equations to yield $5x = 100$, and $x = 20$.

19. **24.** Let the number of rocks $= n$. If 5 rocks are left over when each student receives 5 rocks, $n = 5s + 5$. If 19 more rocks are needed to give each student 6 rocks, $6s = n + 19$, and $6s - 19 = n$. Thus, $5s + 5 = 6s - 19$, and $24 = s$.

20. **D.** If $5p - 1 \geq 9$, $5p \geq 10$, and $p \geq 2$. Thus, the least possible value of p is 2 and the least possible value of $p + 3$ is $2 + 3 = 5$.

21. **8.** $-10x + 28 = 4x$, $28 = 14x$, and $2 = x$. Thus, the maximum value of x is 2. Plug in 2 for x into one inequality to find the maximum value of y. The maximum value of y is $4(2) = 8$.

22. $0 < x < .7$ **or** $0 < x < \frac{7}{10}$. When $a = 0$, x and y both equal 0. Since $a > 0$, y must be greater than 0. When $a = \frac{1}{5}$, $2x = \frac{1}{5}$, and $x = \frac{1}{10}$. Thus, $\frac{1}{10} + y = 4(\frac{1}{5})$, and $y = \frac{7}{10}$. Since $a < \frac{1}{5}$, x is smaller than $\frac{1}{10}$, and y is smaller than $\frac{7}{10}$, or .7.

23. **C. D.** A must be greater than 200. Rearrange the equation to determine $R = 1.2 - .001A$. Since $R > .6$, substitute $1.2 - .001A$ for R. Thus, $1.2 - .001A > .6$, $.6 > .001A$, and $600 > A$.

24. **17.** If the vendor buys 10 bags of tilapia and x bags of catfish, he spends $10(\$14) + 21x$ dollars. The total amount spent must be less than or equal to $500. $10(14) + 21x \leq 500$, $140 + 21x \leq 500$, $21x \leq 360$, and $x \leq 17.1$. At most 17 bags can be bought to fulfill the price constraints. The total weight of 10 bags of tilapia and x bags of catfish is at most 150. $10(4) + 3x \leq 150$, $40 + 3x \leq 150$, $3x \leq 110$, and $x \leq 36.67$. At most 36 bags can be bought without violating the weight constraint. The greatest solution to both inequalities is 17. If between 18 and 36 are bought, the price requirement is violated.

25. **D.** The height is greater than 4. If $2h + d = 25$, $d = 25 - 2h$. If $d \geq 7$, substitute $25 - 2h$ for d. $25 - 2h \geq 7$, $18 \geq 2h$, and $9 \geq h$. If h is greater than 9, then d is less than 7, which is unacceptable. For example, if $h = 10$, $2(10) + d = 25$, $20 + d = 25$, and $d = 5$.

26. **28.** $200 \div 7 \approx 28.57$. Only 28 children can receive 7 red marbles as needed for a full set. $121 \div 3 = 40\frac{1}{3}$. Up to 40 children can receive 3 blue marbles as needed for a full set. However, only 28 can receive all 10 (7 red and 3 blue).

27. **5.** For 200 flags, $200 \times 5 = 1,000$ feet of green fabric needed. If it is sold in packs of 15 feet, $1000 \div 15 = 66\frac{2}{3}$, so 67 bulks of 15 feet are needed. $67 \times 15 = 1005$, and $1005 - 1000 = 5$ feet of green fabric left over. $200 \times 3 = 600$ feet of white fabric needed. $600 \div 3 = 200$ feet with nothing left over.

133

28. **167, 168, 169, and 170.** Let the number of small boxes equal x and the number of large boxes equal y. Since there are 200 boxes, $x + y = 200$. The total weight of the boxes can be represented by $5x + 10y = 1150$ if the weight is at its smallest possible value. To solve for x, multiply the first equation by -10 to yield $-10x - 10y = -2000$ and add that to the second equation to yield $-5x = -850$, and $x = 170$. If the boxes weigh 1165 pounds, then the second equation is $5x + 10y = 1165$. Multiply the first equation by -10 to yield $-10x - 10y = -2000$ and add it to the second equation to yield $-5x = -835$, and $x = 167$. Thus, there can be 167, 168, 169, or 170 small boxes.

29. **D.** If $\frac{2}{3}$ of a cup of sweet potatoes has 76 calories, $\frac{1}{3}$ of a cup has $\frac{76}{2} = 38$ calories and a full cup has $38 \times 3 = 114$ calories. Let the number of cups of carrots $= c$ and the number of cups of sweet potatoes $= s$. $c + s = 2$ and $52c + 114s = 135$. Multiply the first equation by -114 to yield $-114c - 114s = -228$. Add the equations together to yield $-62c = -93$, and $c = 1.5$.

30. **C.** $\frac{5}{3}$ is the slope, the change in height per year. Thus, n is the age and a is the height. For example, when $n = 3$, the height is 5 since $\frac{5}{3}(3) = 5$. When $n = 6$, the height is 10, since $\frac{5}{3}(6) = 10$.

Week 4

1. **54.** There are 12 inches in a foot, so 1,800 feet= $1800 \times 12 = 21{,}600$ inches. The number of boxes that can be wrapped is $21{,}600 \div 400 = 54$ boxes.
2. **B.** The ratio of the diameter of the smaller pulley to the bigger one is 100:200, or 1:2. The ratio of the rpm of the smaller pulley to the bigger one must be 2:1. Thus, set a proportion to find the rpm of the larger pulley. $\frac{2}{1} = \frac{300\ rpm}{x\ rpm}$, $2x = 300$, and $x = 150$.
3. **A.** Speed= $\frac{distance}{time} = \frac{15t^2}{t} = 15t$.
4. **1980.** $120\ \cancel{rods} \times \frac{1\ \cancel{league}}{960\ \cancel{rods}} \times \frac{3\ \cancel{miles}}{1\ \cancel{league}} \times \frac{5280\ feet}{1\ \cancel{mile}} = 1980$ feet.
5. **1361.** $40\ \cancel{talents} \times \frac{75\ \cancel{pounds}}{1\ \cancel{talent}} \times \frac{453.6\ \cancel{grams}}{1\ \cancel{pound}} \times \frac{1\ kilogram}{1000\ \cancel{grams}} = 1360.8$ kilograms, which rounds to 1361 kilograms.
6. **30.** $3\ \cancel{furlongs} \times \frac{660\ \cancel{feet}}{1\ \cancel{furlong}} \times \frac{1\ \cancel{yard}}{3\ \cancel{feet}} \times \frac{1\ chain}{22\ \cancel{yards}} = 30$ chains.
7. **A.** $\frac{\$3}{1\ \cancel{gallon}} \times \frac{1\ \cancel{gallon}}{30\ miles} = \frac{1}{10}$ of a dollar per mile. To find how many miles= 24 dollars, set the equation $\frac{1}{10}m = 24$.
8. **B.** The number of gallons used per hour is $\frac{1\ gallon}{27\ \cancel{miles}} \times \frac{50\ \cancel{miles}}{1\ hour} = \frac{50}{27}$ gallons per hour. The number of gallons left after h hours is $12 - \frac{50}{27}h$.
9. **C.** $3\ \cancel{hours} \times \frac{40\ \cancel{miles}}{1\ \cancel{hour}} \times \frac{1\ gallon}{25\ \cancel{miles}} = 4.8$ gallons, which rounds to 5 gallons.
10. **52.5.** $\frac{103.25\ miles}{118\ minutes} \times \frac{60\ minutes}{1\ hour} = 52.5$ miles per hour.
11. **24.** $\frac{18.4\ miles}{46\ miles\ per\ hour} = .4$ hours, which is equivalent to $.4 \times 60 = 24$ minutes.
12. **36.** The total distance is $5.2 + 6.8 + 9.6 = 21.6$ miles and the total time is $8.4 + 9.7 + 17.9 = 36$ minutes. His average speed in miles per hour is $\frac{21.6\ miles}{36\ \cancel{minutes}} \times \frac{60\ \cancel{minutes}}{1\ hour} = 36$ miles per hour.
13. **29.** $\frac{19.6\ miles}{40\ miles\ per\ hour} = .49$ hours, which is equivalent to $.49 \times 60 = 29.4$ minutes. To the nearest whole number, this is 29 minutes.
14. **A.** $\frac{680{,}000{,}000\ miles}{1\ \cancel{year}} \times \frac{1\ \cancel{year}}{365\ \cancel{days}} \times \frac{1\ \cancel{day}}{24\ hours} \approx 77{,}625$, which rounds to 78,000 miles per hour.
15. **B.** Let the number of males equal $3x$ and the number of females= $4x$. $3x + 4x = 139, 7x = 139$, and $x \approx 19.85$, which we can round to 20. $3x = 3(20) = 60$, which is closest to 59.
16. **324.** Let the number of males= $18x$ and the number of females= $81x$. $18x + 81x = 396, 99x = 396$, and $x = 4$. Thus, the number of females is $81(4) = 324$.
17. **D.** Make y the same in both ratios by converting each ratio to an equivalent ratio. Multiplying the first ratio by 4 yields 20:12 and the multiplying the second by 3 yields 12:33. Thus, $x:y:z$ is 20:12:33, and $x:z$ is 20:33.

18. **B.** The ratio is smallest when the rise is small as it can be and the run is large as it can be (the difference between them is greatest, so the rise is the smallest fraction of the run). The ratio is highest when the value of the rise and run are closest together, meaning the ratio is closest to $\frac{1}{1}$. This occurs when the rise is as large as it can be the run is as small as it can be. The lowest possible ratio is $\frac{8}{18} = \frac{4}{9}$. Thus, $\frac{1}{3}$ is too small. The highest possible ratio is $\frac{10}{16} = \frac{5}{8}$. Thus, $\frac{2}{3}$ and $\frac{7}{9}$ are too big. Only $\frac{3}{5}$ is acceptable.

19. **B.** The equation of the line is $y = 3x$ since it runs through the origin and y is three times x. The ratio of b to a is equivalent to 3 to 1.

20. **A.** The slope is the rate of change, which in this case is change in height divided by change in time. In other words, it is the ratio between the growth in centimeters and the number of days passed.

21. **C.** 3 ~~hours~~ × $\frac{60 \ \cancel{minutes}}{1 \ \cancel{hour}}$ × $\frac{300 \ \cancel{characters}}{1 \ \cancel{minute}}$ × $\frac{1 \ word}{5 \ \cancel{characters}}$ = 10,800 words.

22. **B.** $\frac{1.92 \times 10^9 \ \cancel{kilocalories}}{1 \ year}$ × $\frac{1 \ square \ meter}{6,000 \ \cancel{kilocalories}}$ = $\frac{3.2 \times 10^5 \ square \ meters}{1 \ year}$.

23. **B.** 2.5×10^8 ~~kilometers~~ × $\frac{1000 \ \cancel{meters}}{1 \ \cancel{kilometer}}$ × $\frac{1 \ \cancel{second}}{2 \times 10^8 \ \cancel{meters}}$ × $\frac{1 \ minute}{60 \ \cancel{seconds}}$ = 21 minutes. The distance in meters is $2.5 \times 10^8 \times 1000 = 2.5 \times 10^{11}$. Divide this by the transmission rate of 2×10^8 to determine that the signal travels in 1,250 seconds, which is about $\frac{1250}{60} = 21$ minutes.

Week 5

1. **C.** David's meal costs $x + 4$ dollars. The total cost of both meals is $2x + 4$. After a 10% tip, the cost is $1.1(2x + 4) = 2.2x + 4.4$. Each person pays half of this, which is $1.1x + 2.2$.
2. **A.** The cost of one pair of jeans and 2 sweaters before the tax is modeled by $d = 34.90 + 2x$. When taxed at 7.5%, the cost is $(1 + .075)(34.90 + 2x)$, so $d = 1.075(34.90 + 2x)$.
3. **10.** Let the number of liters in the 60% solution= x. Thus, $.3(5) + .6x$ is the total number of liters of salt. The total number of liters of solution is $x + 5$. If the solution is 50% salt, then there is $.5(x + 5)$ liters of salt. Thus, $.3(5) + .6x = .5(x + 5), 1.5 + .6x = .5x + 2.5, .1x = 1$, and $x = 10$.
4. **13.5.** Let the entire budget= x. The budget for utilities is $.3(.45)x = .135x$, which is 13.5% of the budget.
5. **32.** Let the number of red apples= $8x$ and the number of green apples= $17x$. Thus, there are $8x + 17x = 25x$ apples. To find what percent are red, $\frac{8x}{25x} \times 100 = 32\%$.
6. **77.2.** Let the number of students= x. There are $.4x$ males and $.6x$ females. $.7(.4x) = .28x$ males have at least one pet and $.82(.6x) = .492x$ females have at least one pet. There are $.28x + .492x = .772x$ people with at least one pet, which is 77.2% of the people.
7. **52.** Let the total number of students= x. If 45% are males, 55% are females. Thus, there are $.45x$ males, and $.4(.45x) = .18x$ who take Italian and $.55x$ females and $.3(.55x) = .165x$ females who take Italian. The percent that are males is $\frac{.18x}{.165x + .18x} = \frac{.18x}{.345x} \times 100 \approx 52\%$.
8. **B.** Let the original price= x. After a 5% tax and a 30% discount, the price is $(1 + .05)(1 - .3x)$. Thus, $(1.05)(.7)x = d$, and $x = \frac{d}{(1.08)(.7)}$.
9. **585.** Let the sum of the other two numbers= n and $x = 1.3n$. Thus, $n + 1.3n = 1035, 2.3n = 1035$, and $n = 450$. Thus, $x = 1.3(450) = 585$.
10. **852.** Let the original price= x. $(1 - .25)(1 - .1)x = 575.10, (.75)(.9)x = 575.10, .675x = 575.10$, and $x = 852$.
11. **2.** Let the number of liters in the 40% solution= x. Thus, there are $.1(4) + .4x$ total liters of sugar. The total number of liters of solution is $x + 4$. If the solution is 20% salt, then there is $.2(x + 4)$ liters of salt. Thus, $.1(4) + .4x = .2(x + 4), .4 + .4x = .2x + .8, .2x = .4$, and $x = 2$.
12. **4600.** Let the mass of the mixture= x. $\frac{1.5}{100} = \frac{69}{x}$, $6900 = 1.5x$, and $x = 4,600$ grams.
13. **B.** The percent increase from 2010 to 2011 is $\frac{10560 - 8800}{8800} \times 100 = 20\%$. The percent increase from 2011 to 2012 is 10%. The new price is $10560(1.1) = \$11,616$.
14. **B.** John makes $90 for the first 10 hours and $10x$ dollars for the additional x hours. If he saves 80% of his earnings, he saves $.8(90 + 10x) = 72 + 8x$. To save $104, $72 + 8x \geq 104, 8x \geq 32$, and $x \geq 4$.
15. **24.** The percent that is green is $100 - 40 - 20 - 15 = 25\%$. If there are x marbles, $\frac{25}{100} = \frac{30}{x}, 25x = 3000x$ and $x = 120$. If 20% of the marbles are red, there are $.2 \times 120 = 24$ red marbles.
16. **C.** $800 \times .2 = 160$ pages printed in 10 minutes, or $160 \div 10 = 16$ pages printed per minute. Thus, 16 fewer pages remain to be printed each minute, and $y = 800 - 16t$.
17. **80.** Let the original price= x. After a 10% discount $x(1 - .1) = 72, .9x = 72$, and $x = 80$.

18. **A.** The amount by which the price exceeds $2,000 is $d - 2000$. For example, if the price is $2,500, then it exceeds $2,000 by $500 since $2,500 - 2,000 = 500$. 8% of $d - 2000$ is $.08(d - 2000)$. Thus, $C(d) = .08(d - 2000)$.

19. **C.** The percent change is $\frac{20-10}{10} \times 100 = \frac{10}{10} \times 100 = 100\%$.

20. **D.** If x is the number of milliliters in the 15% solution and y is the number of milliliters in the 30% solution, $x + y = 10$. The amount of sugar is $.15x + .30y$. If 24% of the $x + y$ milliliters are sugar, there are $.24(x + y)$ milliliters of sugar.

21. **B.** The distance of a seat from the ground increases and then decreases in a cyclical manner.

22. **78.** The amount of money in the account after 10 years is $50(1 + .045)^{10} \approx 77.65$, which rounds to 78 dollars.

23. **D.** When a quantity increases by a constant multiplier over time (in this case by a factor of 3), the relationship is exponential. In exponential models, quantities increase by a constant percent of their current value. In this case, the constant percent is 200%. When the constant percent is $r\%$, $1 + \frac{r}{100}$ =the constant multiplier. Thus, $1 + \frac{r}{100} = 3, \frac{r}{100} = 2$, and $r = 200\%$.

24. **70.** She pays $\frac{2}{3}(\$60) = \$40$ for the blouse. She pays $.8x$ for the bag if it costs x dollars. The total price after the tax is $1.08(40 + .8x)$. Thus, $1.08(40 + .8x) = 103.68, 40 + .8x = 96, .8x = 56$, and $x = 70$.

Week 6

1. **C.** 5.25 is the slope, the <u>predicted/expected</u> (not necessarily actual) increase in y (grade) when x (study time in hours) increases by 1.
2. **C.** The model shows that a person who studies 20 hours can be expected to earn a score of 152, which is not a possible grade. Thus, the model does not do a good job predicting the grade for a person who studies 20 hours.
3. **D.** The y-intercept shows the expected value of y (grade) when x (study time) is 0. The actual grade that any student who does not study earn might vary from this amount.
4. **C.** The greatest number of hours for which a person used the phone and still had a battery life at or above 4 hours was 6 hours. However, this person had less battery life than was predicted by the line of best fit. The next highest person used the phone for 5 hours and had a battery life that was greater than that predicted by the line of best fit (the line predicted about 5.25 hours of battery life even though 6 actual hours were left).
5. $\frac{5}{13}$. 5 out of 13 points are below the line of best fit, meaning the line overestimated them.
6. $\frac{1}{3}$. $\frac{90 \, Factory \, A}{270 \, Total} = \frac{1}{3}$ of the units.
7. **B.** The probability of a Factory C widget being Widget R is $\frac{50}{80} = \frac{5}{8}$ and the probability of a Factory B widget being Widget R is $\frac{60}{100} = \frac{3}{5}$. To find how many times more likely the first outcome is, divide the probabilities. $\frac{5}{8} \div \frac{3}{5} \cong 1.04$.
8. **A.** Of the 50 people who used program A, 35 improved.
9. **A.** Of the 35 students who did not improve, 20 used program B.
10. **3.** The percent who improved from A is $\frac{35}{50} \times 100 = 70\%$. The percent who improved from B is $\frac{55}{75} \times 100 = 73.33\%$, about a 3% difference.
11. $\frac{7}{11}$. Out of the 11 people who prefer prose, 7 prefer fiction.
12. $\frac{5}{9}$. Out of the 9 people who prefer nonfiction, 5 prefer poetry.
13. **51.** The red die landed on an even number 51 out of 100 times, or 51% of the times.
14. **B.** The points form a straight line. Pick a point that is approximately along the line of best fit, such as (5,13). Mass=Density×Volume, $13 = d(5)$, and $2.6 = d$. The density of glass (2.58) is closest to this value.
15. **C.** Pick any two numbers on the plot. When the mass is 10 kilograms, the weight is about 90 Newtons. $90 \div 10 = 9$ as the acceleration due to gravity, which is closest to that of Saturn.
16. **C.** The slope is the ratio between the weight (y) and the mass (x), which is the acceleration due to gravity, (acceleration due to gravity=$\frac{Weight}{Mass}$).
17. **55.** $49 = 9.8m$, and $5 = m$. Thus, the weight on Neptune is $5(11) = 55$ newtons.
18. **B.** Chocolate and strawberry are the only two flavors for which more second graders prefer them to first graders. Thus, $y > x$ for these values, so the data points will appear above $y = x$.
19. $\frac{6}{7}$. Of the 7 people who scored a 1, 6 were in group 1 or 2.
20. **30.** 18 out of 60 people received a 4. $\frac{18}{60} \times 100 = 30\%$.
21. **C.** Of the 46 people who scored at least 2 (greater than or equal to 2), 15 were in Group 3.

22. **20.** 96 total people support the measure ($24 + 72 = 96$) and 84 oppose it ($65 + 19 = 84$). Thus, the difference is 12 people. If x total people in the town support the measure, $\frac{12}{180} = \frac{x}{300}$, $180x = 3600$, and $x = 20$. Note that since the question asks for the answer in thousands, 300 can be used in the proportion ($300{,}000 = 300$ groups of $1{,}000$).

Week 7

1. **90**. The sum of the first 10 scores is $10 \times 85 = 850$. The sum of all 20 scores is $20 \times 92 = 1840$. The sum of the last 10 ratings is $1840 - 850 = 990$. If ratings 12 through 20 are as large as they can be, the 11th is small as it can be. If ratings 12 through 20 are each 100, there sum is $100 \times 9 = 900$. Thus, the 11th rating must be $990 - 900 = 90$ for the sum to be 990.
2. **49**. The sum of the 6 players' scores is $24 \times 6 = 144$ and the sum of the 5 remaining players' is $19 \times 5 = 95$. The highest-scoring player earned $144 - 95 = 49$ points.
3. **95**. The sum of the first 4 scores is $90 \times 4 = 360$. The sum of all 5 scores must be $91 \times 5 = 455$. Thus, the last score must be $455 - 360 = 95$.
4. **B**. Since the average is higher than the median, there must be some high outliers. Thus, a few cars are valued higher than the rest.
5. **2.75**. The sum of the scores in Group 2 is $7(4) + 6(3) + 3(2) + 3(1) + 1(0) = 55$. The average is $55 \div 20 = 2.7$.
6. **C**. The median is the average of the tenth and eleventh scores, which is 3 for both groups.
7. **13**. The average mass of Sherilynn's rocks $\frac{1.7+2.9+1.8+3.6+4}{5} = 2.8$. The average of Pippa's must be 4.8. $\frac{3+2.7+1.1+4.2+x}{5} = 4.8$, $11 + x = 24$, and $x = 13$.
8. **B**. $x = \frac{p+10}{2}$ and $y = \frac{3p+14}{2}$. The average of x and y is $\frac{x+y}{2} = \frac{\frac{p+10}{2}+\frac{3p+14}{2}}{2} = \frac{\frac{4p+24}{2}}{2} = \frac{2p+12}{2} = p+6$.
9. **A**. The grades for Class A are more spread out, so the standard deviation is higher.
10. **C**. The median of 21 terms is the term in the $\frac{21+1}{2} = 11^{th}$ position. The 11th highest number of representatives in the table is 13.
11. **D**. The average is $\frac{10+28+42+x}{4} > 30$, which is rearranges into $10 + 28 + 42 + x > 4(30)$.
12. **3**. The median is the average of the 200th and 201st student. Students 1 to 30 took 4 courses. Students 31 to 210 took 3, so 3 is the median.
13. **C**. The median is the average of the middle two terms. $\frac{13200+13600}{2} = 13400$.
14. **D**. The percent of the sample of eels with 0 to 9 plates should be around equal to that of the population of eels.
15. **4320**. The candidate should get at least $52\% - 4\% = 48\%$ of the vote. $9{,}000 \times .48 = 4{,}320$.
16. **D**. The sample is biased because subjects are not chosen randomly amongst the whole city population. Golfers are likely to have different opinions than general residents.
17. **D**. The measure will likely get between 46 and 52 percent of the vote (3 percent above or below 49%). Thus, the results are too close to call.
18. **C**. Measure C should get between 43 and 51 percent of the vote (4 percent above or below 47%). Therefore, the measure may or not pass. A and D are expected to pass because even the lower end of the margin of error is above 50%. B is expected to fail because even the upper end of the margin of error is below 50%. There is most uncertainty about C.
19. **C**. Surveys can only show correlation, but not cause and effect because subjects are not assigned treatments randomly. The correlation only applies to the population studied (women).
20. **B**. Conclusions about cause and effect can be drawn since the subjects were randomly assigned to groups. However, the results cannot be generalized to all adults since volunteers were used (subjects must be chosen randomly for the experiment in order to make such generalizations).

21. **C.** About 34% of the points below the mean and 34% of the points above the mean should be within one standard deviation. $83 \times .34 = 28$ people. Below the mean, the number of people in classes 2-5 (32 people total) is close to this value. Above the mean, the number of people in classes 6-9 (26 people total) is also close to this value. The standard deviation estimated from the upper end is somewhere between $125,000 - 72,000 = 53,000$ and $139,999 - 72,000 = 67,999$. On the lower end, the estimated standard deviation is between $72,000 - 34,999 = 37,001$ and $72,000 - 25,000 = 47,000$. 50,000 is the only choice within the estimated range.
22. **C.** The actual percent is likely, but not guaranteed, to be within 3.2% points of 30%. Since 25% is well below the range included in the margin of error (26.8% − 33.2%), it is unlikely the true number is less than this percent.
23. **A.** There ae 41 terms, so the median is the 21st highest ($41 + 1 = 42$ and $42 \div 2 = 21$). The median is 85, the high is 100, and the low is 55. Eliminate choice D, which shows the low score as 35. The third quartile is the median of the top 20 grades, which is 90 (the average of the 10th and 11th highest). The first quartile is the median of the bottom 20 grades, which is 75 (the average of the 10th and 11th lowest), as in A.
24. **D.** A larger sample size causes the margin of error to decrease. Thus, there may have been more females in the study.

Week 8

1. **B.** Rewrite 27^b as 3^{3b}. Thus, $\frac{3^a}{27^b} = \frac{3^a}{3^{3b}} = 3^{a-3b} = 3^{10}$.
2. **C.** $3^{\frac{3}{2}} = \sqrt{3^3} = \sqrt{27} = \sqrt{9} \cdot \sqrt{3} = 3\sqrt{3}$.
3. **D.** $8^{\frac{4}{5}} = 2^{3(\frac{4}{5})} = 2^{\frac{12}{5}} = \sqrt[5]{2^{12}}$.
4. **C.** $4^{\frac{3}{4}} = 2^{2(\frac{3}{4})} = 2^{\frac{3}{2}} = \sqrt{2^3} = \sqrt{8} = \sqrt{4} \cdot \sqrt{2} = 2\sqrt{2}$.
5. **C.** $\sqrt[3]{a^7} \times \sqrt[4]{a^3} = a^{\frac{7}{3}} \cdot a^{\frac{3}{4}} = a^{\frac{28}{12}} \cdot a^{\frac{9}{12}} = a^{\frac{37}{12}}$.
6. **2.** $\sqrt[5]{a} \times \sqrt[5]{a^9} = a^{\frac{1}{5}} \cdot a^{\frac{9}{5}} = a^{\frac{10}{5}} = a^2$.
7. **B.** By the power rule, $(25x^2)^{\frac{1}{2}} = 25^{\frac{1}{2}} \cdot x^{2 \cdot \frac{1}{2}} = 5|x|$.
8. **C.** $x^{\frac{1}{2}} = \sqrt{x}$. By negative exponent rules, $x^{-2} = \frac{1}{x^2}$ and $\frac{1}{y^{-3}} = y^3$. Thus, $\frac{x^{-2}}{x^{\frac{1}{2}}y^{-3}} = \frac{y^3}{x^2\sqrt{x}}$.
9. **D.** Since $(x^6)^5 = x^{30}, n = (2)^5 = 32$.
10. **D.** $(a + \frac{b}{4})^2 = (a + \frac{b}{4})(a + \frac{b}{4}) = a^2 + \frac{ab}{4} + \frac{ab}{4} + \frac{b^2}{16} = a^2 + \frac{ab}{2} + \frac{b^2}{16}$.
11. **B.** $y^{\frac{1}{4}} \cdot y^2 = y^{\frac{1}{4}+2} = y^{\frac{1}{4}+\frac{8}{4}} = y^{\frac{9}{4}}$. Thus, $n = 9$.
12. **C.** By the power rule, $(x^3y^4)^{\frac{1}{3}} \times (x^3y^4)^{\frac{1}{4}} = x^1y^{\frac{4}{3}} \cdot x^{\frac{3}{4}}y^1$. By the product rule, add exponents of like bases. $= x^{(1+\frac{3}{4})} \cdot y^{(\frac{4}{3}+1)} = x^{(\frac{4}{4}+\frac{3}{4})} \cdot y^{(\frac{4}{3}+\frac{3}{3})} = x^{\frac{7}{4}}y^{\frac{7}{3}}$. Thus, $n = 7$.
13. **D.** $\frac{x^3}{x^6} = x^{-3} = \frac{1}{x^3}$ and $\frac{y^{\frac{3}{2}}}{y} = \frac{y^{\frac{3}{2}}}{y^{\frac{2}{2}}} = y^{\frac{1}{2}} = \sqrt{y}$. Thus, $\frac{x^3y^{\frac{3}{2}}}{x^6y} = \frac{\sqrt{y}}{x^3}$.
14. **A.** $4x + 16y = 4(a^2 + 4b^2) + 16ab = 4a^2 + 16b^2 + 16ab$. Recognize that $4a^2 + 16ab + 16b^2$ is a sum the perfect trinomial taking the form $(x + y)^2 = x^2 + 2xy + y^2$. In this case, $4a^2$ acts as x^2, so x is $2a$, and $16b^2$ acts as y^2, so $4b$ is y. You can also confirm that $(2a + 4b)^2 = 4a^2 + 16ab + 16b^2$.
15. **A.** $(3x - 4)(x^2 + 2x + 5) = 3x(x^2 + 2x + 5) - 4(x^2 + 2x + 5) = 3x^3 + 6x^2 + 15x - 4x^2 - 8x - 20 = 3x^2 + 2x^2 + 7x - 20$.
16. **B.** $\frac{1}{2}x^2 - 5 = \frac{1}{2}(x^2 - 10) = \frac{1}{2}(x - \sqrt{10})(x + \sqrt{10})$.
17. **C.** $\sqrt{(p-n)^3} \cdot \sqrt{(p-n)} = \sqrt{(p-n)^4} = (p-n)^2 = p^2 - 2pn + n^2$.
18. **D.** $(16x)^a = 2x^a, 16^a \cdot x^a = 2x^a, 16^a = 2, 2^{4a} = 2^1, 4a = 1$, and $a = \frac{1}{4}$.
19. $\frac{1}{2}$ or .5. $\frac{\sqrt{98}-\sqrt{50}}{2} = \frac{\sqrt{49}\cdot\sqrt{2}-\sqrt{25}\cdot\sqrt{2}}{2} = \frac{7\sqrt{2}-5\sqrt{2}}{2} = \frac{2\sqrt{2}}{2} = \sqrt{2}$, which is equal to $2^{\frac{1}{2}}$. Thus, $a = \frac{1}{2}$.
20. **C.** $(-2x^3)^{\frac{4}{3}} = (-2)^{\frac{4}{3}}(x^3)^{\frac{4}{3}} = \sqrt[3]{2^4}x^4 = \sqrt[3]{16}x^4 = \sqrt[3]{8} \cdot \sqrt[3]{2} \cdot x^4 = 2x^4\sqrt[3]{2}$.
21. **B.** $\sqrt[4]{x^{12a}y^3} = (x^{12a})^{\frac{1}{4}}(y^3)^{\frac{1}{4}} = x^{3a}y^{\frac{3}{4}}$.
22. **D.** $(36x^{16}y^7)^{\frac{1}{2}} = 36^{\frac{1}{2}} \cdot x^{\frac{16}{2}} \cdot y^{\frac{7}{2}} = 6x^8y^{\frac{7}{2}}$.
23. **A.** $(x^3)^2 = (x^{48})^n, x^6 = x^{48n}, n = \frac{6}{48}$, and $n = \frac{1}{8}$.
24. **D.** $(1.6x - 2.2)^2 - (1.5x - 6.2) = 2.56x^2 - 7.04x + 4.84 - 1.5x + 6.2 = 2.56x^2 - 8.54x + 11.04$.
25. **10.** $25x^4 - 9y^2 = (5x^2 - 3y)(5x^2 + 3y), 80 = 8(5x^2 + 3y)$, and $10 = 5x^2 + 3y$.

143

26. **B.** $R = (40 - .02x)x = 40x - .02x^2$. Thus, $P = -.02x^2 + 40x - (.10x^3 + .02x^2 + 2x + 10)$, $P = -.02x^2 + 40x - .10x^3 - .02x^2 - 2x - 10$, and $P = -.10x^3 - .04x^2 + 38x - 10$.

27. **B.** Factor by grouping. $2x^3 + bx^2 + 6x + 3b = x^2(2x + b) + 3(2x + b) = (x^2 + 3)(2x + b)$. $2x + b$ is a factor.

28. **B.** $\frac{1}{x^{\frac{b}{5}}} = x^{\frac{-b}{5}}$. Thus, $\frac{-b}{5} = 4, -b = 20$, and $b = -20$. $\frac{3b}{4} = \frac{3(-20)}{4} = -15$.

29. **C.** $\sqrt[n]{3^{3n} \cdot 2^{n+5}} = \sqrt[n]{3^{3n}} \cdot \sqrt[n]{2^n \cdot 2^5} = 3^{\frac{3n}{n}} \cdot 2^{\frac{n}{n}} \cdot \sqrt[n]{2^5} = 3^3 \cdot 2\sqrt[n]{32} = 54\sqrt[n]{32}$. You can also plug in a real number for n into both the original expression and the answer choices to confirm that choice C has the same value.

Week 9

1. **10.** $\frac{x^2+7x-30}{x-a} = \frac{(x+10)(x-3)}{(x-3)} = x + 1$, so $a = 10$.
2. **B.** Multiply the numerator and each fraction in the denominator by the common denominator $(x - 3)(x + 4)$. $\frac{1(x-3)(x+4)}{\frac{1(x-3)(x+4)}{x-3}+\frac{1(x+4)(x-3)}{x+4}} = \frac{x^2+x-12}{x+4+x-3} = \frac{x^2+x-12}{2x+1}$.
3. **D.** $\frac{x^3-16x}{x^2-7x+12} = \frac{x(x^2-16)}{(x-4)(x-3)} = \frac{x(x-4)(x+4)}{(x-4)(x-3)} = \frac{x(x+4)}{x-3}$.
4. **B.** $(-12x - 7)(ax - 1) + 66 = 24x^2 + 26x + 73$, and $-12ax^2 - 7ax + 12x + 7 + 66 = 24x^2 + 26x + 73$. Thus, $-12ax^2 = 24x^2$, and $a = -2$.
5. **B.** $(-24x - 13)(ax - 1) + 2 = 48x^2 + 50x + 15$, $-24x^2 - 13ax + 24x + 13 + 2 = 48x^2 + 50x + 15$. Thus, $-24ax^2 = 48x^2$, and $a = -2$.
6. **C.** The remainder is 74 so the quotient is $7x + 14 + \frac{74}{2x-4}$.

$$\begin{array}{r} 7x+14 \\ 2x-4 \overline{\smash{)}14x^2 +18} \\ -(14x^2 - 28x) \\ \hline 28x + 18 \\ -(28x - 56) \\ \hline 74 \end{array}$$

7. **B.** First simplify the expression. Split the linear term in the numerator into two terms that add to 8 but multiply to equal -48 since $3 \times 16 = -48$. 12 and -4 are such terms. Thus, $3x^2 + 8x - 16 = 3x^2 + 12x - 4x - 16$. Now, we can factor by grouping. $3x^2 + 12x - 4x - 16 = 3x(x + 4) - 4(x + 4) = (3x - 4)(x + 4)$. The denominator factors into $(4 - x)(4 + x)$ by difference of perfect squares. Thus, $\frac{3x^2+8x-16}{16-x^2} = \frac{(3x-4)(x+4)}{(4-x)(4+x)} = \frac{3x-4}{4-x} = \frac{3x-4}{-x+4}$. Now we can do long division. The remainder is 8 and the quotient is -3, so $-3 + \frac{8}{-x+4}$ is correct.

$$\begin{array}{r} -3 \\ -x+4 \overline{\smash{)}3x-4} \\ -(3x - 12) \\ \hline 8 \end{array}$$

8. **D.** $f(0) = 2 - g(0)$, and $g(0) = 3(0) - 1 = -1$. Thus, $f(0) = 2 - (-1) = 3$.
9. **45.** First set $x - 3$ equal to 2 to yield $x = 5$. Then plug in 5 for x to $7(5) + 10 = 35 + 10 = 45$.
10. **B.** $f(2) + g(2) = 5 + (-3) = 2$.
11. **A.** $\frac{3}{x-2} + \frac{6}{3(x-2)} = \frac{9}{3(x-2)} + \frac{6}{3(x-2)} = \frac{15}{3(x-2)} = \frac{5}{x-2}$.
12. **C.** $\frac{1}{\frac{1}{x+2}+\frac{1}{x+5}} = \frac{1(x+5)(x+2)}{\frac{1(x+5)(x+2)}{(x+2)}+\frac{1(x+5)(x+2)}{(x+5)}} = \frac{x^2+7x+10}{2x+7}$.
13. **1.** $\frac{2a+3}{(a+1)^2} - \frac{2}{a+1} = \frac{2a+3}{(a+1)^2} - \frac{2(a+1)}{(a+1)^2} = \frac{2a+3-2(a+1)}{(a+1)^2} = \frac{2a+3-2a-2}{(a+1)^2} = \frac{1}{(a+1)^2}$.

14. **B.** Find the slope using two sets of points from the table. $\frac{8-(-4)}{2-0} = \frac{12}{2} = 6$. As x increases by 1, $f(x)$ increases by 6. Thus, $f(3) = 8 + 6 = 14$.

15. **A.** According to the graph, n is 3 (the maximum height). According to the table $G(3) = 1$.

16. **3 or 6.** Plug $h - 4$ in for n. $(h - 4 - 2)(h - 4 + 1)^3 = 0$, and $(h - 6)(h - 3)^3 = 0$. Thus, $h = 6$ or $h = 3$.

17. **B.** $x^2 - 8x + 16 = (x - 4)^2$. Thus, $(x + a + 1)^2 = (x - 4)^2$, $(x + a + 1) = x - 4$, $x + a = x - 5$, and $a = -5$.

18. **17.** The slope of $f(x)$ is $\frac{6-2}{1-0} = 4$. Thus, the slope of $g(x)$ is 2. Since $g(0) = 1$, the y-intercept of g is 1 and $g(x) = 2x + 1$. Thus, $g(8) = 2(8) + 1 = 16 + 1 = 17$.

19. **12.** Pick any two points on the line. The line includes (0,3) and (4,5), so the slope of $f(x)$ is $\frac{5-3}{4-0} = \frac{2}{4} = \frac{1}{2}$. The slope of $g(x)$ is $4(\frac{1}{2}) = 2$. The y-intercept is -8, so $g(x) = 2x - 8$ and $g(10) = 2(10) - 8 = 20 - 8 = 12$.

20. **201.** First find the slope of the function. $\frac{5-3}{2-1} = 2$. Since $f(1) = 3, f(0) = 3 - 2 = 1$. The y-intercept is 1 and $f(x) = 2x + 1$. Thus, $f(100) = 2(100) + 1 = 200 + 1 = 201$.

21. **A.** $G(x) = (-64)^3$ and $f((-64)^3) = \sqrt[3]{-64^3} = (-64^3)^{(\frac{1}{3})} = -64$.

22. **2.** Plug some coordinates for x into the original equation. Some points on the graph of $f(x)$ include (0,3), (1,0), and (2,-1). The graph above includes the points (2,3), (3,0) and (4,-1). Thus, $f(x - h)$ is the graph of $f(x)$ shifted 2 units right, so $h = 2$. You can also determine that the axis of symmetry of the original function is $x = \frac{-(-4)}{2(1)} = 2$. The axis of symmetry in the graph is $x = 4$, representing a shift of 2 to the right.

23. **B.** $F(1) = 8$ and $G(1) = 3$.

24. **15.** $7 = \frac{(12-a)^2+164}{2(12)}, 7 = \frac{(x-a)^2+164}{24}, 168 = (12 - a)^2 + 164, 4 = (12 - a)^2, 2 = (12 - a)$, and $a = 10$. Thus, $f(6) = \frac{(6-10)^2+164}{2(6)} = \frac{16+164}{12} = 15$.

25. **C.** Plug in $x + a$ for x into the function.
$$3(x + a)^2 - 7 = 3x^2 + 12x + 5$$
$$3(x^2 + 2ax + a^2) = 3x^2 + 12x + 12$$
$$3x^2 + 6ax + 3a^2 = 3x^2 + 12x + 12$$
$$6ax + 3a^2 = 12x + 12$$
Equate linear terms and constant terms. Thus, $6ax = 12x$, and $a = 2$. Also, $3a^2 = 12, a^2 = 4$, and $a = \pm 2$. Only 2 is a solution to both equations.

Week 10

1. **A.** Rearrange the equation to yield $2x^2 - 5x - p = 0$. The discriminant must be negative if there are no real solutions. $(-5)^2 - 4(2)(-p) < 0, 25 + 8p < 0, 8p < -25p$, and $p < \frac{-25}{8}$. Only A is less than this value.
2. **8.** The discriminant must equal 0. $b^2 - 4(2)(8) = 0, b^2 - 64 = 0, b^2 = 64$, and $b = 8$.
3. **D.** The polynomial can further be factored into $(p-2)(p+2)(p+3)(p+3)$. If $p - 2 = 0, p = 2$ is a factor. If $p + 2 = 0, p = -2$ is a factor. If $p + 3 = 0, p = -3$ is a factor.
4. **B.** Multiply all terms by 2 to yield $2x^2 + kx + 8p = 0$. By the quadratic formula, $x = \frac{-k \pm \sqrt{k^2 - 4(2)(8p)}}{2(2)} = \frac{-k \pm \sqrt{k^2 - 64p}}{4}$.
5. **1.** $x^5 - 3x^3 + 2x = 0, x(x^4 - 3x^2 + 2) = 0, x(x^2 - 2)(x^2 - 1) = 0$. Thus, $x = 0$, which we are told is unacceptable. If $x^2 - 2 = 0, x^2 = 2$, and $x = \pm\sqrt{2}$, which are not integers. If $x^2 - 1 = 0, (x-1)(x+1) = 0$, and $x = 1$ or $x = -1$. 1 is the only positive integer solution.
6. **D.** $(ax + 3)(bx + 7) = 18x^2 + cx + 21$, and $abx^2 + 7ax + 3bx + 21 = 18x^2 + cx + 21$. Thus, $ab = 18$. If $a + b = 9$, then a and b must be 6 and 3. $7ax + 3bx = cx$. When $a = 6$ and $b = 3$, $7(6)x + 3(3)x = 42x + 9x = 51x$. When $a = 3$ and $b = 6, 7(3)x + 3(6)x = 21x + 18x = 39x$. Thus, $c = 39$ or 51.
7. **A.** Divide all terms by 3. $y = x^2 + 3x + 1$. By the quadratic formula, $x = \frac{-3 \pm \sqrt{3^2 - 4(1)(1)}}{2(1)} = \frac{-3 \pm \sqrt{5}}{2} = \frac{-3}{2} \pm \frac{\sqrt{5}}{2}$.
8. **1 or 2.** $x(x^4 - 5x^2) = -4x, x^5 - 5x^3 = -4x, x^5 - 5x^3 + 4x = 0, x(x^4 - 5x^2 + 4) = 0, x(x^2 - 4)(x^2 - 1)$. If $x^2 - 4 = 0, x^2 = 4$, and $x = \pm 2$. If $x^2 - 1 = 0, x^2 = 1$, and $x = \pm 1$. The positive values are 1 or 2.
9. **6.** Factor by grouping. $x^3 - 6x^2 + 2x - 12 = 0, x^2(x-6) + 2(x-6)$, and $(x^2 + 2)(x - 6) = 0$. Thus, $x - 6 = 0$, and $x = 6$. The other solutions are imaginary roots. If $x^2 + 2 = 0, x^2 = -2$, and $x = \pm i\sqrt{2}$.
10. **A.** $x - 3 = \frac{5}{x-3}, (x-3)^2 = 5$, and $x - 3 = \sqrt{5}$.
11. **D.** $b^2 - 4(16)(64) > 0, b^2 - 4096 > 0, b^2 > 4096$, and $b > 64$. 70 is acceptable.
12. **C.** $\sqrt{x + 15} = x + 3, x + 15 = x^2 + 6x + 9, x^2 + 5x - 6 = 0$, and $(x-1)(x+6) = 0$. If $x - 1 = 0, x = 1$ and if $x + 6 = 0, x = -6$. Test each solution $\sqrt{1 + 15} = 1 + 3, \sqrt{16} = 4$, and $4 = 4$. Thus, 1 is a real solution. $\sqrt{-6 + 15} = -6 + 3, \sqrt{9} = -3$, and $3 \neq -3$. -6 is extraneous.
13. **B.** $\sqrt{x - 5} = x - 7, x - 5 = x^2 - 14x + 49, x^2 - 15x + 54$, and $(x-9)(x-6) = 0$. If $x - 9 = 0, x = 9$ and if $x - 6 = 0, x = 6$. Test each solution. $\sqrt{9 - 5} = 9 - 7, \sqrt{4} = 2$, and $2 = 2$. Thus, 9 is a solution. $\sqrt{6 - 5} = 6 - 7, \sqrt{1} = -1$, and $1 \neq -1$. 6 is an extraneous solution.
14. **8.** Raise each side to the third power. $\sqrt[3]{8r} = \frac{1}{2}r, 8r = \frac{1}{8}r^3, 64r = r^3, 64 = r^2$, and $8 = r$.
15. **B.** Set the equations equal to each other. $-18x^2 + 2 = 18x^2 - 2, 4 = 36x^2, \frac{1}{9} = x^2$, and $x = \pm \frac{1}{3}$. Thus, $k = \frac{1}{3}$.

16. **D.** The x-coordinate of the vertex is the mean of the roots. If $x - 4 = 0, x = 4$ and if $x + 6 = 0, x = -6$. The mean of the roots is $\frac{4+(-6)}{2} = \frac{-2}{2} = -1$. Thus, d, the y-coordinate of the vertex, is $a(-1-4)(-1+6) = a(-5)(5) = -25a$.
17. **C.** Since there is a root at $x = -2$, $x + 2$ is a factor. Since there is a root at $x = 1$, $x - 1$ is a factor. Since the graph changes directions at $x = 1$, there is a double zero so $(x-1)^2$ is a factor.
18. **A.** The function has a y-intercept of 0. Eliminate C and D, which have y-intercepts (constant terms) of -2 and 2. The function has zeros at $x = 0, x = -1$, and $x = -2$. For choice A, factor out an x. $x(x^2 + 3x + 2) = x(x+1)(x+2)$. For choice B, factor out a $-x$. $-x(x^2 + 3x + 2) = -x(x+1)(x+2)$. Both functions have the correct zeros. To determine which is the correct answer, test a point on the graph, such as (1,5). In choice A, when $x = 1, y = 5$ and in choice B, when $x = 1, y = -5$. Choice A is correct.
19. **D.** There is only 1 positive real root. A and B are incorrect because they include the real negative root -2. According to the graph, when $x = 0, y$ is positive. In choice C, when $x = 0, y = -2$, so C is incorrect. In choice D, when $x = 0, y = 2$, which could be correct.
20. **3.** The roots are at $x = -2$ since if $x + 2 = 0, x = -2$ and $x = 8$ since if $x - 8 = 0, x = 8$. The x-coordinate of the vertex is the mean of the roots. $\frac{-2+8}{2} = 3$.
21. **D.** The domain includes all values for which $-2x$ is greater than or equal to 0, which occurs when x is <u>less than</u> or equal to 0 since the product of two negative numbers is positive.
22. **C.** The expression must be factorable by factoring by grouping. Factoring x^2 out of the first two terms, yields $x^2(x-3)$. If $t = 48, -16x + 48$ can factor into $-16(x-3)$. Thus, $x^2(x-3) - 16(x-3)$ becomes $(x^2 - 16)(x-3)$, which further factors into $(x-4)(x+4)(x-3)$.
23. **49.** $\sqrt{xy+2} = 3, xy + 2 = 9, xy = 7$, and $x^2y^2 = 49$.
24. **169.** $x^4 + 2x^2y^2 + y^4 = (x^2+y^2)^2 = 13^2 = 169$.
25. **D.** $4a - 12b = 20z, 4(a-3b) = 20z$, and $a - 3b = 5z$. Since $a^2 - 6ab + 9b^2 = (a-3b)^2$, it also equals $(5z)^2 = 25z^2$.
26. **A.** $4b$ is negative, and the real solution to the radical equation cannot be negative.
27. **B.** $y = a(x-h)^2 + k$ is the vertex form for a parabola with vertex (h,k). The vertex is (3,7) since the sign after x is opposite that of the x-coordinate of a parabola for an equation in vertex form. Since the coefficient of a is negative, the parabola opens downward.
28. **B.** Since the parabola opens down, the coefficient of the squared term is negative. Since the y-intercept is positive, the constant term is positive.
29. **A.** The roots are $x = -5$ since if $x + 5 = 0, x = -5$ and $x = -3$ since if $x + 3 = 0, x = -3$. The x-coordinate of the vertex is halfway between these values.
30. **C.** $(x-2)(x^2 - 6x + 8) = (x-2)(x-2)(x-4)$. There are two zeros at $x = 2$ since if $x - 2 = 0, x = 2$ and one at $x = 4$ since if $x - 4 = 0, x = 4$. Thus, there are two distinct (different) zeros.
31. **D.** An equation with no real zeros has no x-intercepts (by definition, x-intercepts are real zeros).
32. **C.** $y = x^2 + 2x + 8$ has no real zeros since the discriminant is negative. $2^2 - 4(1)(8) = 4 - 32 = -28$.
33. **B.** The y-intercepts are the points at which $x = 0$. B puts the equation in factored form to reveal y-intercepts at $y = 4$ and $y = -2$.
34. **A.** The x-intercept is the point at which $y = 0$. In choice A, this is -8.
35. **D.** The function is undefined when the denominator is 0. D puts the denominator in factored form to reveal these points.

36. **D.** The x-coordinate of the vertex is the mean of the roots. The roots are 6 and -2, and the average of 6 and -2 is $\frac{6+(-2)}{2} = \frac{4}{2} = 2$. The vertex of A is $(2-6)(2+2) = (-4)(4) = -16$. The vertex of B is $.5(-16) = -8$. The vertex of C is $2(-16) = -32$. The vertex of D is $-10(-16) = 160$. D is farthest.

37. **25.** 100 out of 350 are males. Let x equal the number of added males. $\frac{100+x}{350+x} = \frac{1}{3}$, $300 + 3x = 350 + x$, $2x = 50$, and $x = 25$.

Week 11

1. **D.** The solution occurs at the point of intersection. $49 = (x-2)^2$, and $\pm 7 = (x-2)$. If $7 = x - 2, 9 = x$ and if $-7 = x - 2, x = -5$. The distance between 9 and -5 is $9 - (-5) = 14$.
2. **C.** $y = (2x-1)(x+2) = 2x^2 + 4x - x - 2 = 2x^2 + 3x - 2$. Thus, if $x = 2y + 1, x = 2(2x^2 + 3x - 2) + 1, x = 4x^2 + 6x - 4 + 1$, and $4x^2 + 6x - 3 = 0$. The discriminant is $6^2 - 4(4)(-3) = 36 + 48 = 84$, which is positive. Thus, there are 2 solutions.
3. **2 or 18.** $-\frac{1}{2}(x-6)^2 + 5 = -4x + 5, -\frac{1}{2}(x-6)^2 = -4x, (x-6)^2 = 8x, x^2 - 12x + 36 = 8x, x^2 - 20x + 36 = 0$, and $(x-18)(x-2) = 0$. Thus, $x - 18 = 0$ and $x = 18$ or $x - 2 = 0$ and $x = 2$.
4. **B.** Substitute $4x$ for y into the first equation. $x^2 + (4x)^2 = 153, x^2 + 16x^2 = 153, 17x^2 - 153 = 0, 17(x^2 - 9) = 0, 17(x-3)(x+3) = 0$. Thus, $x = 3$ or -3. If $x = -3, y = 4(-3) = -12$.
5. **21.** If $6x - 2$ is a factor, then set $6x - 2$ equal to 0 to find the x-intercept. $6x - 2 = 0, 6x = 2$, and $x = \frac{1}{3}$. Thus, $f(\frac{1}{3}) = 0, 18(\frac{1}{3})^2 - \frac{1}{3}c + 5 = 0, 18(\frac{1}{9}) - \frac{1}{3}c + 5 = 0, 2 - \frac{1}{3}c + 5 = 0, 7 - \frac{1}{3}c = 0, 7 = \frac{1}{3}c$, and $21 = c$.
6. **7.** By the remainder theorem, the remainder when $f(x)$ is divided by x (the equivalent of $x - 0$), is $f(0)$, which is 7.
7. **C.** By the remainder theorem, the remainder when $f(x)$ is divided by $x - 1$ is 3 when $f(1) = 3$.
8. **4.** By the factor theorem, if $x - 3$ is a factor, $y = 0$ when $x = 3$. $0 = 3^3 - 2(3)^2 - 3c + 3, 0 = 27 - 18 - 3c + 3, 0 = -3c + 12, -3c = -12$, and $c = 4$.
9. **D.** If $2x - 1$ is a factor, then it has an x-intercept when $2x - 1 = 0$. Thus, $2x = 1$, and $x = \frac{1}{2}$. $f(\frac{1}{2}) = 2(\frac{1}{2})^3 - (\frac{1}{2})^2 + 1 = 2(\frac{1}{8}) - \frac{1}{4} + 1 = \frac{1}{4} - \frac{1}{4} + 1 = 1$. $g(\frac{1}{2}) = -\frac{1}{2}$. Thus, $f(x) + 2g(x)$ is a factor of $p(x)$ since $1 + 2(-\frac{1}{2}) = 1 + (-1) = 0$.
10. **3.4 or $\frac{17}{5}$.** $2(x^2 + 3x + 1) + 5(3x + k) = 2x^2 + 6x + 2 + 15x + 5k = 2x^2 + 21x + 2 + 5k$. If $x + 1$ is a factor, $f(-1) = 0$. $2(-1)^2 + 21(-1) + 2 + 5k = 0, 2 - 21 + 2 + 5k = 0, -17 = -5k$, and $\frac{17}{5} = k$.
11. **B.** Since there is an x-intercept at $x = 40$, $x - 40$ is a factor by the factor theorem.
12. **B.** Since (10,300) is on the graph, the remainder is 300 when the function is divided by $x - 10$ by the remainder theorem.
13. **A.** Rearrange the linear equation to yield $y = -2n - a$ and set $-2n - a$ equal to $ax^2 + n$ to yield $ax^2 + a + 3n = 0$. To find the number of solutions, find the discriminant. $0^2 - 4a(a + 3n) = -4a^2 - 12an$. If a and n are both positive, the discriminant is negative. For example, if a and n are both 1, the discriminant is $-4 - 12 = -16$. Thus, there are no solutions, or no points of intersection.
14. **B.** C cannot be correct because if $b = 0$, the vertex would be on the y-axis. Since there are no real x-intercepts, the discriminant must be negative, as in choice B. $(-3)^2 - 4(2)(5) = -31$. A and D each have two solutions since their discriminants are positive.

15. **4**. Let there be x friends originally. Each friend pays $\frac{200}{x}$. After one friend joins each pays $\frac{200}{x+1}$. Since the original cost is $10 more, $\frac{200}{x} = \frac{200}{x+1} + 10$, $\frac{200(x+1)\cancel{(x)}}{\cancel{x}} = \frac{200\cancel{(x+1)}(x)}{\cancel{x+1}} + 10(x+1)(x)$, $200x + 200 = 200x + 10(x^2 + x)$, $200x + 200 = 200x + 10x^2 + 10x$, $10x^2 + 10x - 200 = 0$, $x^2 + x - 20 = 0$, $(x+5)(x-4) = 0$, and $x = -5$ or $x = 4$. There must be 4 friends (reject negative answer). $200 \div 4 = \$50$ per friend originally and $200 \div 5 = \$40$ after one more person joins.

16. **5**. The cost per each friend originally is $\frac{600}{x}$. After one friend backs out, the cost for each remaining friend is $\frac{600}{x-1}$. Since each friend now pays $30 more, $\frac{600}{x} + 30 = \frac{600}{x-1}$, $\frac{600\cancel{(x)}(x-1)}{\cancel{x}} + 30(x)(x-1) = \frac{600(x)\cancel{(x-1)}}{\cancel{x-1}}$, $600(x-1) + 30(x)(x-1) = 600x$, $600x - 600 + 30(x^2 - x) = 600x$, $600x - 600 + 30x^2 - 30x = 600x$, $30x^2 - 30x - 600 = 0$, $x^2 - x - 20 = 0$, $(x-5)(x+4) = 0$. If $x - 5 = 0$, $x = 5$ and if $x + 4 = 0$, $x = -4$. There must be 5 friends (reject the negative answer). $\$600 \div 5 = \$120$ a person originally and $\$600 \div 4 = \$150$ a person after one person drops out, a $30 increase.

17. **B**. When a horizontal line is drawn at $y = -4$, the line intersects the function 3 times, so there are 3 solutions.

18. **44**. Let width$= w$ and length$= w + 8$. Since the area is 105, $(w+8)(w) = 105$, $w^2 + 8w = 105$, $w^2 + 8w - 105 = 0$, $(w+15)(w-7) = 0$. Thus, $w + 15 = 0$, and $w = -15$ and $w - 7 = 0$, and $w = 7$. Reject the negative solution, so $w = 7$ and length$= 7 + 8 = 15$. The perimeter is $2(7) + 2(15) = 14 + 30 = 44$.

19. **16**. Let x equal the number of price changes. The price after x price changes of $2 is $24 - 2x$ and the number of shirts sold with each price change is $20 + 5x$. Thus, revenue$= (24 - 2x)(20 + 5x)$. To find the number of price changes that maximizes the revenue, take the mean of the roots. If $24 - 2x = 0$, $24 = 2x$, and $12 = x$. If $20 + 5x = 0$, $20 = -5x$, and $-4 = x$. The mean of the roots is $\frac{12-4}{2} = 4$. 4 price changes maximize the revenue, so the new price is $24 - 2(4) = 24 - 8 = \$16$.

20. **110**. The initial height is 110, the y-intercept.

21. **1.25**. The time at which the maximum height is reached is $\frac{-40}{2(-16)} = 1.25$.

22. **135**. The maximum height is $-16(1.25)^2 + 40(1.25) + 110 = 135$.

23. **46**. By the vertex formula, $y = a(x-h)^2 + k$ the maximum speed occurs at 46 (the number subtracted from x). Note that 48 is the maximum gas mileage.

24. **C**. If $y - 1 = x$, then $y = x + 1$. Thus, the solutions occur when $-x^2 + 2x + 7 = x + 1$, and $x^2 - x - 6 = 0$. Thus, $(x-3)(x+2) = 0$, and $x = 3$ and $x = -2$. If $y - 1 = 3$, $y = 4$, so $(3,4)$ is a solution. If $y - 1 = -2$, $y = -1$, so $(-2, -1)$ is a solution.

25. **C**. The graph of $f(x)$ is wider, so $c < d$.

26. **D**. The width is $x - 5$, so area is $x(x-5) = x^2 - 5x$.

27. **11**. $2(x^2 + ax) + 4(ax^2 + 3x) = 2x^2 + 2ax + 4ax^2 + 12x$. Thus, $2x^2 + 4ax^2 = 0$ and $2ax + 12x = bx$, $2x^2 + 4ax^2 = 0$, and $2x^2(1 + 2a) = 0$. Thus, $1 + 2a = 0$, $1 = -2a$, and $-\frac{1}{2} = a$. Thus, $2(-\frac{1}{2})x + 12x = bx$, $-x + 12x = bx$, $11x = bx$, and $11 = x$.

151

Week 12

1. **A.** The increase in population is exponential such that the original value is 3. The percent increase is $.13\% = .0013$. Thus, $P = 3(1 + .0013)^t$, and $P = 3(1.0013)^t$.
2. **D.** A coordinate on $f(x)$ is $2^0 + 2 = 1 + 2 = 3$. Thus, (0,-3) is a coordinate on $-f(x)$.
3. **D.** The decay factor is .8 since the population decreases by 20% and $1 - .2 = .8$. Since the decrease happens every 3 years, the $\frac{1}{3}$ of a 20% cycle happens per year, so $f(n) = 50,000(.8)^{\frac{n}{3}}$.
4. **C.** The original equation shows that the increase is 5% per year. In one quarter of a year, one fourth of a 5% increase cycle occurs, so $S = 2000(1.05)^{\frac{q}{4}}$.
5. **C.** In one minute, one fourth of a doubling cycle occurs. In one hour $\frac{1}{4} \times 60 = 15$ doubling cycles occur. Thus, $y = 50(2)^{15x}$.
6. **B.** $BC = AB + A, BC - AB = A, B(C - A) = A$, and $B = \frac{A}{C-A}$.
7. **C.** If $3\sqrt{4x} = n$, then $\sqrt{4x} = \frac{n}{3}$. Square both sides to determine that $4x = \frac{n^2}{9}$.
8. **C.** In one minute, $\frac{1}{16}$ of a tripling cycle occurs. In one hour, $60 \times \frac{1}{16} = \frac{15}{4}$ of a cycle occurs. Thus, $y = 4(3)^{\frac{15h}{4}}$.
9. **B.** $\frac{a-b}{b} = \frac{4}{9}, 9(a-b) = 4b, 9a - 9b = 4b, 9a = 13b$, and $\frac{a}{b} = \frac{13}{9}$.
10. **A.** $\frac{x}{y} = x + z, x = y(x + z), x = xy + yz, x - xy = yz, x(1 - y) = yz$, and $x = \frac{yz}{1-y}$.
11. **36.** $4a^2b^2c^2 = 64, a^2b^2c^2 = 16, \sqrt{a^2b^2c^2} = \sqrt{16}$, and $abc = 4$. Thus, $9abc = 9(4) = 36$.
12. **B.** The value is the y-intercept, the average cost when $x = 0$, or in the year 2005.
13. **B.** Each year the average housing cost goes up by a factor of 1.025, so 2 years later it goes up by 1.025^2.
14. **C.** Profits go up by 7% every 4 years, or 48 months.
15. **.56.** $r = 1 - .44 = .56$.
16. **251.** $800(.56)^2 = 250.88$, which rounds to $251.
17. **70.** The relationship between time and money is exponential. Since after 3 years there are $560 and the amount of money doubles each year, $x(2)^3 = 560, 8x = 560$, and $x = 70$.
18. **D.** The graph is exponential. Since the exponent is negative, the function is decreasing. You can confirm this by plugging in values for a and b graphing the equation. Suppose $a = 1$ and $b = -2$. When $x = 1, y = 1$ but when $x = 2, y = \frac{1}{4}$.
19. **D.** Let the kinetic energy for the slower car$=\frac{1}{2}mv^2$. Let the kinetic energy for the faster car$=\frac{1}{2}m(3v)^2 = \frac{9}{2}mv^2$. Thus, the kinetic energy of the faster car in 9 times that of the smaller, so the KE equals $30,000 \times 9 = 270,000$.
20. **C.** Substitute $2xy$ for S in the second equation. $V = \frac{2xy^2}{5}, 5V = 2xy^2$, and $\frac{5V}{2y^2} = x$.
21. **A.** $q = \frac{1}{2}nv^2, 2q = nv^2, \frac{2q}{n} = v^2$, and $\sqrt{\frac{2q}{n}} = v$.
22. **A.** $\frac{\sqrt{yz}}{20} = \frac{4+y}{60}, 60(\sqrt{yz}) = 20(4 + y), \sqrt{yz} = \frac{20(4+y)}{60}$, and $\sqrt{yz} = \frac{4+y}{3}$.

152

23. **.4 or $\frac{2}{5}$.** If (c, d) is a point on $y = 3x + b$, then $d = 3c + b$. If $(2c, 3d)$ is a point on $y = 4x + b$, then $3d = 4(2c) + b$, and $3d = 8c + b$. Rearranging each equation, $d - 3c = b$ and $3d - 8c = b$. Thus, $d - 3c = 3d - 8c, 2d = 5c$, and $\frac{2}{5} = \frac{c}{d}$.

24. **D.** The number doubles each day. Thus, the equation $y = 1.5 \times 10^5(2)^x$ models the number bacteria where x is the number of days AFTER day 1. Thus, $1.5 \times 10^5(2)^{x-1}$ represents the number of bacteria on any given day. On day 1, there are $1.5 \times 10^5(2)^{1-1} = 1.5 \times 10^5$. On day 2, there are $1.5 \times 10^5(2)^{2-1} = 3 \times 10^5$. On Day 11, there are $1.5 \times 10^5(2)^{11-1} = 1.536 \times 10^8$. You can also confirm by making a table of values. Doubling 1.5×10^5 ten times will yield 1.536×10^8.

25. **C.** The equation must be exponential since the temperature does not change by a constant. Plug in any value from the table to see that C is correct rather than D. For example, $20 + 185(.93)^0 = 20 + 185 = 205$.

26. **B.** The simplest strategy is to plug in real numbers. If m and k each equal 1, $T = 2\pi$. The doubled period is 4π. Since the new spring constant is still 1, to solve for the new mass, $2\pi\sqrt{\frac{m}{1}} = 4\pi, \sqrt{m} = 2$, and $m = 4$. The ratio is 4 to 1. To solve algebraically, let the original mass equal m_1 and the second mass equal m_2. Let the original period equal T_{s1}, and $T_{s1} = 2\pi\sqrt{\frac{m_1}{k}}$. Let the second period equal T_{s2}. $T_{s2} = 2\pi\sqrt{\frac{m_2}{k}}$. Since the period is doubled, $T_{s2} = 2(2\pi\sqrt{\frac{m_1}{k}}) = 4\pi\sqrt{\frac{m_1}{k}}$. To find the relationship between the masses, $2\pi\sqrt{\frac{m_2}{k}} = 4\pi \times \sqrt{\frac{m_1}{k}}, \sqrt{\frac{m_2}{k}} = 2 \times \sqrt{\frac{m_1}{k}}$ (dividing both sides by 2π), $\frac{m_2}{k} = \frac{4m_1}{k}, km_2 = 4km_1$, and $m_2 = 4m_1$.

Week 13

1. **12.** The figure consists of three similar triangles since the bases are all parallel to each other. The ratio of the height of the middle level to the height of the entire structure must be $\frac{3x}{4x+3x+x} = \frac{3x}{8x} = \frac{3}{8}$. If the height of the structure is 32 feet, the height of the middle level is $32 \times \frac{3}{8} = 12$.
2. **9.** By Pythagorean triplets, $BC = 3$. Triangles ABC and EDC are similar since AB and DE are parallel. Thus, $\frac{BC}{CD} = \frac{AB}{ED}, \frac{3}{CD} = \frac{4}{16}, 48 = 4CD$, and $12 = CD$. Since $CB + BD = 12, BD = 9$.
3. **B.** By the triangle inequality theorem, the second side can be 10 and third must be less than the sum of the first two sides. $10 + 10 = 20$, and 19 is the largest possible integer value of the third side. Thus, the largest possible perimeter is $10 + 10 + 19 = 39$.
4. **A.** Triangles EFG and FHG are similar since both have angle G and a 32-degree angle. Therefore, $\frac{HG}{FH}$ is equal to $\frac{FG}{EF}$ since HG and FG are opposite 32-degree angles and FH and EF are opposite angle G.
5. **B.** The ratio between the segments formed by an angle bisector can be related by the angle bisector theorem. When bisector AD is drawn to segment BC, $\frac{BD}{DC} = \frac{AB}{AC}$.
6. **8.** Triangles EDC and ABC are similar. Let the length of $CD = x$ and the length of $BD = 3x$ (if CD is $\frac{1}{3}$ the length of BD, then BD is three times length of CD). Thus, the ratio of CD to BC is $x:(x + 3x) = x:4x = 1:4$. Since BC is 4 times the length of CD, AB is 4 times the length of ED, and $2 \times 4 = 8$.
7. **D.** The width is $l - 4$. The perimeter is $2l + 2(l - 4) = 2l + 2l - 8 = 4l - 8$.
8. **8.** The triangle is a 30-60-90 right triangle. Let the smallest side$= x$, the middle side$= x\sqrt{3}$, and the longest side$= 2x$. $x + x\sqrt{3} + 2x = 12 + 4\sqrt{3}$, and $x = 4$, so the longest side is $2(4) = 8$.
9. **21.** If AB is parallel to CD, triangles ABE and DCE are similar. The ratio of AB:CD is $30:40 = 3:4$. Thus, the ratio of AE to ED is also 3:4. Let $AE = 3x$ and $ED = 4x$. Thus, $3x + 4x = 49, 7x = 49$, and $x = 7$. Thus, $AE = 3(7) = 21$.
10. **81.** Let the length of each side of the square$= x$ and the length of each side of the triangle$= x + 3$. The perimeters are equal since the rods used to make them have the same length, so $4x = 3(x + 3), 4x = 3x + 9$, and $x = 9$. Thus, the area of the square is $9^2 = 81$ square feet.
11. **B.** Side AB must equal 8. $6^2 + AB^2 = 10^2, 36 + AB^2 = 100, AB^2 = 64$, and $AB = 8$. If $DE = 24$, then each side of triangle DEF is three times that of the corresponding side in ABC. Thus, $EF = 6 \times 3 = 18$. Area$= \frac{1}{2} \times 18 \times 24 = 216$.

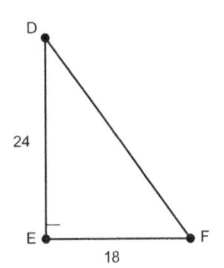

12. **A.** Each exterior angle of the hexagon is 360 ÷ 6 = 60 degrees. Thus, each smaller right triangle is a 30-60-90 right triangle. The ratio between the sides of 30-60-90 right triangles is $x : x\sqrt{3} : 2x$. AF, BC, CD, and FE correspond to $2x$ and each have a length of 6. JE, DH, IA, and BG each correspond to x and have a length of 3. IF, FJ, GC, and CH each correspond to $x\sqrt{3}$ have a length of $3\sqrt{3}$. The base of the rectangle= $3 + 6 + 3 = 12$ and the width= $3\sqrt{3} \times 2 = 6\sqrt{3}$. The area is $12 \times 6\sqrt{3} = 72\sqrt{3}$.

13. **C.** Use 30-60-90 triangle ratios to find the missing sides. The area is $10.5 \times 7\sqrt{3} = 73.5\sqrt{3}$.

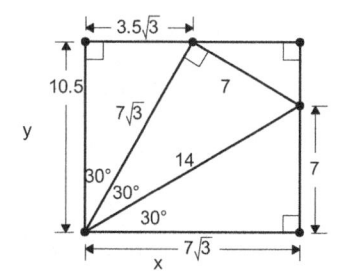

14. **A.** Since BDEF is a square, BF and DE are parallel, ADE is similar to ABC (they are both right triangles with common angle A), and EFC is similar to ABC (they are both right triangles with common angle C). Let each side of the square= n. If the ratio of AB:BC is 3:4, $AB = \frac{3}{4}BC$ and $BC = \frac{4}{3}AB$. Likewise, AD is $\frac{3}{4}DE$, or $\frac{3}{4}n$ and FC is $\frac{4}{3}EF$, or $\frac{4}{3}n$. The area of triangle ABC is $\frac{1}{2}\left(\frac{3}{4}n + n\right)\left(\frac{4}{3}n + n\right) = \frac{1}{2}\left(\frac{7}{4}n\right)\left(\frac{7}{3}n\right) = \frac{49}{24}n^2$. The area of the square is n^2. To find what fraction the area of the square is of the area of the triangle, divide the area of the square by the area of the triangle. $\frac{n^2}{\frac{49n^2}{24}} = \frac{24}{49}$.

15. **C.** The triangle exists since the sum of any two sides is greater than the third. The sum of the squares of the smaller sides is less than the square of the third. $3^2 + 4^2 = 25$, which is less than $6^2 = 36$. Thus, the triangle is obtuse. When the sum of squares of the smaller sides equals the square of the larger, the triangle is a right triangle. When the sum is smaller, it is obtuse. When it is larger, it is acute.

16. **36.** Adjacent angles along a line are supplementary. $(2x + 6) + (3x + 9) + 3(2x) = 180$, $11x + 15 = 180, 11x = 165$, and $x = 15$. Thus, angle $ABG = 2(15) + 6 = 36$.

17. **58.** Because angles AED and BED are supplementary, $2x + 11 + x - 5 = 180$, $3x + 6 = 180, 3x = 174$, and $x = 58$.

18. **50.** By the vertical angles theorem, angle CEA equals angle DEB. If $x = 58$, angle CEA= $58 - 5 = 53$ and angle FEB= $58 + 19 = 77$. Since angles CEA, FEB, and CEA (y) are adjacent angles along a line, $53 + 77 + y = 180$, and $y = 50$.

19. **D.** By the vertical angles theorem, q must equal t, r must equal u, and s must equal v. Let the measure of q and $t = x$, r and $u = y$, and s and $v = z$. If $q + r = s + t, x + y = z + x$. If y added to x is the same as z added to x, $y = z$. Thus, angles $r, u, s,$ and v are all equal.

20. **D.** The alternate interior angles are not equal, so the lines intersect.

21. **C.** If angle 1= angle 3, then lines l and k are parallel since corresponding angles are congruent.

22. **8.** By alternate interior angles, $3x = 24$, so $x = 8$.

23. **148.** Since the sum of the angles of a triangle is 180, $x + 3x + y = 180, 8 + 24 + y = 180$, and $y = 148$.
24. **50.** Angle AHI is corresponding to the 130-degree angle. Angle BHI is supplementary to angle AHI since these angles are a linear pair. Thus, angle BHI= 50 degrees since $180 - 130 = 50$. Since angle BIH is the third angle of triangle BHI, let the angle equal x. $x + 80 + 50 = 180$, and $x = 50$.
25. **10.** Since the sum of the angles in a triangle is 180, angle AHB equals 60 and angle FHE equals 50. By vertical angles, angle AHG= 50 as well. Since angles along a line are supplementary, $60 + 50 +$ angle $GHC = 180$, and angle $GHC = 70$. Since the interior angles of triangle GHC add to 180 degrees, $70 + 100 + x = 180$, so $x = 10$.
26. **75.** Alternate interior angles are congruent. Angle x and the 75-degree angle are alternate interior angles.
27. **50.** The sum of the angles of triangle is 180. If $x = 75, 75 + 55 + y = 180$, and $y = 50$.
28. **70.** Angle EDF is supplementary to 125 degrees, 125 +angle $EDC = 180$, and angle EDC= 55. Since $ED = EF$, angle EFD also equals 55 degrees. Since the sum of the angles in a triangle is 180, $55 + 55 + x = 180$, and $x = 70$.
29. **$19 < x < 25$.** The third side must be greater than $22 - 3 = 19$ and less than $22 + 3 = 25$.
30. **49.** The largest possible value of the third side is less than $10 + 15$, or 25. Thus, the largest possible integer value is 24. The largest the perimeter can be is $24 + 15 + 10 = 49$.
31. **22.** The sum of n and n must be greater than 10. If $2n > 10, n > 5$. The smallest possible perimeter is $2(6) + 10 = 22$.
32. **47.** By the vertical angles theorem, angle AEB measures 90 degrees. There are 180 degrees in triangle AEB. If angle B equals x degrees, $43 + 90 + x = 180$, and $x = 47$.
33. **A.** Since the triangles are similar, the bases of the triangles are parallel.
34. **35.** By alternate interior angles, $x = 35$ and $y = 25$. Angle E in each triangle equals 120, since $120 + 25 + 35 = 180$.
35. **60.** DE and AC are corresponding since they are opposite angle B, and BD and BC are corresponding because they are opposite right angles. Therefore, triangles ABC and EBD are similar, and BE corresponds to AB. $\frac{AC}{DE} = \frac{AB}{BE}, \frac{AC}{8} = \frac{15}{2}$, $2AC = 120$, and $AC = 60$.
36. **C.** Angle x equals 40 degrees by the vertical angles theorem. Angle D and x are congruent alternate interior angles. Thus, the segments are parallel.
37. **1.** DE and AC are corresponding since they are opposite angle B, and BD and BC are corresponding because they are opposite right angles. Therefore, triangles ABC and EBD are similar and BE corresponds to AB. $\frac{DE}{AC} = \frac{BE}{AB}, \frac{x}{7} = \frac{x+1}{14}$, $14x = 7x + 7, 7x = 7$, and $x = 1$.
38. **30.** The triangles are similar because they both have a right angle and angle C. Thus, angle E equals angle A. Sides AC and EC correspond because they are opposite right angles. Sides ED and AB are corresponding because they are opposite angle C. Thus, sides DC and AB are also corresponding. $\frac{EC}{AC} = \frac{ED}{AB}, \frac{15}{AC} = \frac{12}{24}$, $12AC = 360$, and $AC = 30$.

39. $\frac{10}{3}$. The triangles are similar since DE is parallel to BC. Sides DE and BC are corresponding since they are opposite angle A. Sides AE and BC correspond since they are opposite right angles. Angle E must equal angle C, so AD corresponds to AB. If $BC = x, AB = x + 10$. $\frac{AD}{AB} = \frac{DE}{BC}, \frac{12}{x+10} = \frac{3}{x}, 12x = 3x + 30, 9x = 30$, and $x = \frac{30}{9} = \frac{10}{3}$.

40. **8.** Triangles DBE, FBG, and ABC are similar. The height of the top level corresponds to the height of the entire triangle. Side DE corresponds to side AC. Let the height of the top level= x. $\frac{x}{24} = \frac{20}{60}, 60x = 480$, and $x = 8$.

41. **360.** The top base has a length of 6 since $2 - (-4) = 6$. Since each box measures 4 feet, the base is $6 \times 4 = 24$ feet. The bottom base has a length of $1 - (-2) = 3$. The length in feet is $3 \times 4 = 12$ feet. The height is $2 - (-3) = 5$. The length in feet is $5 \times 4 = 20$. The area is $\frac{20(12+24)}{2} = \frac{20(36)}{2} = \frac{720}{2} = 360$ square feet.

42. **C.** $x^2 + AB^2 = (x+2)^2, x^2 + AB^2 = x^2 + 4x + 4, AB^2 = 4x + 4$, and $AB = \sqrt{4x+4}$.

43. **25.** $CD^2 = 12^2 + 9^2, CD^2 = 225$, and $CD = 15$. BE corresponds to CE because they are opposite equal angles. CD and AB correspond because they are opposite vertical angles. $\frac{CE}{BE} = \frac{CD}{AB}, \frac{12}{20} = \frac{15}{AB}, 12AB = 300$, and $AB = 25$.

44. $\frac{8}{5}$ **or 1.6.** By 8:15:17 triangles, $IF = 15$. Since IF corresponds to HF (they are opposite corresponding angles) and JH corresponds to EI (they are opposite angle F), $\frac{HF}{IF} = \frac{JH}{EI}, \frac{3}{15} = \frac{JH}{8}, 15JH = 24$, and $JH = \frac{24}{15} = \frac{8}{5}$.

45. **C.** If perimeter= 18, side= $18 \div 3 = 6$ since all sides are equal. Area = $side^2 \times \frac{\sqrt{3}}{4}, A = 6^2 \times \frac{\sqrt{3}}{4}$, and $A = 9\sqrt{3}$.

46. **100.** If the side of the hexagon equals x, $\frac{6(x)^2\sqrt{3}}{4} = 150\sqrt{3}, 6x^2\sqrt{3} = 600\sqrt{3}, x^2 = 100$, and $x = 10$. Thus, the area of the square is $10^2 = 100$.

47. **B.** The triangle is an isosceles triangle, so AD and DC each equal 5. $BD^2 + 5^2 = 8^2, BD^2 = 39$, and $BD = \sqrt{39}$.

48. **B.** Angle D= 60 degrees since consecutive angles of parallelograms are supplementary. A 30-60-90 triangle can be drawn. By 30-60-90 ratios, AD is twice DE, so $DE = 2$ and height $AE = 2\sqrt{3}$. The area is $(2\sqrt{3})(20) = 40\sqrt{3}$.

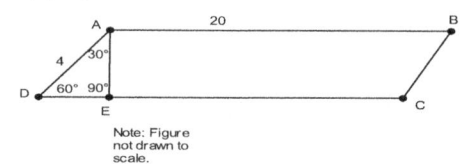

157

49. **B.** Angle D equals 45 degrees since consecutive angles are supplementary. Thus, a 45-45-90 triangle can be drawn. If the area of the parallelogram is 60, the height= 5 since $12h = 60$, and $h = 5$. By 45-45-90 ratios, AD must equal $5\sqrt{2}$.

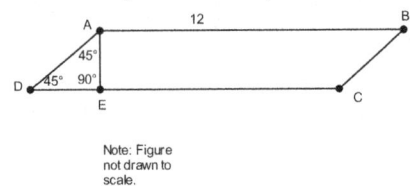

Note: Figure not drawn to scale.

50. **10.** The shape can be broken down into a rectangle and a 45-45-90 triangle. If $BC = 4\sqrt{2}$, the height is 4. Thus, $BE = 4$. The area of triangle BEC is $\frac{1}{2} \times 4 \times 4 = 8$. If the area of the whole figure is 48, the area of the rectangle is $48 - 8 = 40$. $AB \times BE = 40$ since length × width= 40. $AB(4) = 40$, and $AB = 10$.

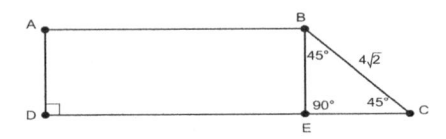

Week 14

1. **D.** $(8-4)^2 + 4^2 = 16 + 16 = 32$, which is larger than 20. Thus, the coordinates are on the exterior of the circle.
2. **A.** The center of the circle is (8,-2). P is 5 to the left of the center, so Q must be 5 to the right of the center, at (13,-2).
3. **C.** 30 is equal to radius squared. $A = \pi r^2 = 30\pi$.
4. **1.** Triangle ABC is a variation of a 5:12:13 right triangle such that each side is divided by 10. Thus, $AB = .5$. The radius is .5, so the diameter is $2 \times .5 = 1$.
5. **C.** Complete the square. $x^2 + 8x + y^2 + 2y = 10$, $x^2 + 8x + (\frac{8}{2})^2 + y^2 + 2y + (\frac{2}{2})^2 = 10 + 16 + 1$, and $x^2 + 8x + 16 + y^2 + 2y + 1 = 27$. Thus, $r^2 = 27$, and $r = \sqrt{27}$.
6. **12.** If $\tan = \frac{4}{3}$, then the reference triangle has an opposite of 4 and an adjacent of 3. Thus, the reference triangle has a hypotenuse of 5. The triangle is a multiple of a 3:4:5 right triangle. Each side is 4 times that of a 3:4:5 right triangle. Since $AC = 4 \times 5$, $BC = 4 \times 3 = 12$.
7. **.8 or $\frac{4}{5}$.** ABC must be a multiple of a 3:4:5 right triangle since $AB = 5 \times 3$ and $BC = 5 \times 4$. Thus, $AC = 5 \times 5 = 25$. Sine D must equal sine A. Sine $A = \frac{BC}{AC} = \frac{20}{25} = \frac{4}{5}$.
8. **0.** Since x and y are complementary, $\cos x = \sin y$, so the difference between them is 0.
9. **C.** $V = \pi r^2 h$. $\pi r^2 = 40$ (the area of the circular base), so the volume of the container $= 40 \times 10 = 400$ cubic centimeters. If the figurine has a volume of 90, then $400 - 90 = 310$ cubic centimeters remaining for the foam.
10. **A.** The area of the base is $(10 - 2x)(5 - 2x) = 4x^2 - 30x + 50$, as shown in choice A. This expression is multiplied by the height, x, to yield the volume.
11. **A.** $\frac{1}{2}(DB)(AC) = 5x^2$, $\frac{1}{2}x(AC) = 5x^2$, $AC = 10x$. Thus, $DC = 10x - x = 9x$. By the Pythagorean Theorem, $x^2 + (9x)^2 = BC^2$, $82x^2 = BC^2$, and $\sqrt{82}x = BC$. Thus, sine of $C = \frac{x}{\sqrt{82}x} = \frac{1}{\sqrt{82}}$.
12. **B.** The line runs through the center of the circle (4,2) since $2 = .5(4)$, so the line divides the circle into two congruent arcs.
13. **A.** Draw a reference triangle with one leg of 5 and a hypotenuse of 13. The triangle must be a multiple of a 5:12:13 right triangle. With respect to angle F, 5 is the opposite and 12 is the adjacent, so $\tan F = \frac{5}{12}$.
14. **44.** $(12 + 2i)(3 - 4i) = 36 - 48i + 6i - 8i^2 = 36 - 42i - 8(-1) = 44 - 42i$. Thus, $a = 44$.
15. **A.** $S = 2Cr$, $S = 2(2\pi r)r$, and $S = 4\pi r^2$. $5.9 \times 10^9 = 4\pi r^2$, $\frac{5.9 \times 10^9}{(4\pi)} = r^2$, and $21668.1121 = r$, which is closest to A.
16. **60.** The circumference of the car is $2(.2)\pi = .4\pi$ meters. If it does 800 revolutions per minute, it does $800 \times 60 = 48,000$ revolutions per hour, for a total distance of $48,000 \times .4\pi = 19,200\pi$ meters. Since there are 1,000 meters in a kilometer, it travels $\frac{19,200\pi}{1,000} = 19.2\pi = 60.3$ kilometers, which rounds to 60.
17. **4.** $\frac{320\pi}{40} = 8\pi$ inches per revolution, which means the circumference is 8π inches. Thus, $2\pi r = 8\pi$, and $r = 4$.

18. **D.** If the radius is 6, then the right side of the equation equals 36 (the radius squared). When (0,0) is plugged into the correct equation, it should equal 36 since (0,0) is on the circle. $(0 - 3\sqrt{2})^2 + (0 + 3\sqrt{2})^2 = 18 + 18 = 36$.

19. **180.** If the area is 144π, $144\pi = \pi r^2$, $144 = r^2$, and $12 = r$. Thus, the diameter is $2(12) = 24$. The age is $7.5(24) = 180$ years old.

20. **B.** $120 = 7.5d$, and $d = 16$ inches, or $\frac{16}{12} = \frac{4}{3}$ feet. Thus, the circumference is $\frac{4}{3}\pi$ feet.

21. **531.** The diameter is now $2(12) = 24$ inches. $a = 7.5(24) = 180$ years old. In 15 years, it will be 195 years old. $195 = 7.5d$, and $d = 26$ inches. Thus, the radius will be 13 inches in 15 years. The area will be $13^2(\pi) \cong 530.93$, which rounds to 531 square inches.

22. **C.** Divide both sides by 2 to yield $x^2 + 5x + y^2 + y = \frac{19}{2}$. Complete the square. $x^2 + 5x + (\frac{5}{2})^2 + y^2 - y + (-\frac{1}{2})^2 = \frac{19}{2} + \frac{25}{4} + \frac{1}{4}, x^2 + 5x + \frac{25}{4} + y^2 - y + \frac{1}{4} = \frac{19}{2} + \frac{25}{4} + \frac{1}{4}, (x + \frac{5}{2})^2 + (y - \frac{1}{2})^2 = 16$. The radius squared is 16, so the radius is 4 and the diameter is 8.

23. **A.** $x^2 + 6x + (\frac{6}{2})^2 + y^2 + 4y + (\frac{4}{2})^2 = 2 + 9 + 4, x^2 + 6x + 9 + y^2 + 4y + 4 = 15, (x + 3)^2 + (y + 2)^2 = 15$. Thus, the center is (-3,-2).

24. **A.** The radius is 2.5 inches. The volume is $\pi(2.5)^2(4) = 25\pi$ cubic inches per cup. $231 \div (25\pi) = 2.94$ cups, so 2 full cups can be filled.

25. **15.** The angles must be complementary if sin x equals cos y. $2k + 10 + 3k + 5 = 90, 5k + 15 = 90, 5k = 75$, and $k = 15$.

26. **7.** $V = \pi r^2 h, 800 = \pi r^2(10)$, and $80 = \pi r^2$. For the second cylinder, $560 = 80h$, and $7 = h$.

27. **720.** The volume of water before the toy is added is $40 \times 30 \times 30 = 36,000$ cubic centimeters. After the toy is added, the volume is $40 \times 30 \times 30.6 = 36,720$ cubic centimeters. The toy has a volume of $36,720 - 36,000 = 720$ cubic centimeters.

28. **15.** If $\cos A = \frac{3}{5}$, ADE and ABC must be multiples of a 3:4:5 triangle. $\tan A = \frac{4}{3}$, so $\sin A = \frac{4}{5}$. $\tan A = \frac{BC}{AB} = \frac{20}{AB}$. Thus, $\frac{20}{AB} = \frac{4}{3}, 60 = 4AB$, and $AB = 15$. If $AB = 15$ and $DB = 6$, then $AD = 15 - 6 = 9$. Each side of ADE is three times a 3:4:5 triangle, so $AE = 5 \times 3 = 15$. Also, $\cos A = \frac{AD}{AE} = \frac{9}{AE}$. If $\cos A = \frac{3}{5}$, then $AE = 15$.

29. **1.** $\frac{3+i}{2-i} \times \frac{(2+i)}{(2+i)} = \frac{6+3i+2i+i^2}{4-i^2} = \frac{6+5i-1}{4-(-1)} = \frac{5+5i}{5} = 1 + i$. Thus, $a = 1$.

30. **2.** $\frac{i^4-9}{i^2-3} = \frac{(i^2-3)(i^2+3)}{i^2-3} = i^2 + 3 = -1 + 3 = 2$.

31. **3.** Chord BC perpendicularly bisects the radius, so h is halfway between 3 and 11. $h = \frac{3+11}{2} = 7$. To solve for k, plug in one point on the circle into the equation. $(x - h)^2 + (y - k)^2 = r^2, (x - 7)^2 + (y - k)^2 = 5^2, (3 - 7)^2 + (0 - k)^2 = 25, 16 + k^2 = 25, k^2 = 9$, and $k = 3$.

32. **A.** The center of the circle must be halfway between the endpoints of the diameter. The x-coordinate is $\frac{-2+8}{2} = 3$ and the y-coordinate is $\frac{-4+4}{2} = 0$. Thus, the equation of the circle is $(x - 3)^2 + y^2 = r^2$, where r is the radius. To find the radius squared, plug in one endpoint. $(8 - 3)^2 + 4^2 = 25 + 16 = 41$. Thus, $(x - 3)^2 + y^2 = 41$. If $(0, p)$ is a point on the circle, $(0 - 3)^2 + p^2 = 41, 9 + p^2 = 41, p^2 = 32$, and $p = \sqrt{32}$.

33. **C.** The center of the circle is (0,0) since $\frac{3+(-3)}{2} = 0$ and $\frac{2+(-2))}{2} = 0$. Thus, $x^2 + y^2 = r^2$. Plug in an endpoint to determine that $r^2 = 13$. For example, $3^2 + 2^2 = 9 + 4 = 13$.

34. **40.** The triangles are similar since AB and DE are parallel. Tan A is equal to tan D since the angles correspond. Tan D= $\frac{EC}{DE}$. Thus, $1.5 = \frac{60}{x}$, $1.5x = 60$, and $x = 40$.

35. **$72 \leq x \leq 78$.** The area of the circle is $4^2\pi = 16\pi$. If the area of the sector= 10, $\frac{10}{16\pi} = \frac{x}{360}$, $3,600 = 16\pi x$, and $71.65 = x$. If the area of the sector= 11, $\frac{11}{16\pi} = \frac{x}{360}$, $3,960 = 16\pi$, and $x = 78.82$. The angle is between 72 and 78 inclusive.

36. **50.** If $QR = 80$, QS and SR each equal 40 since a chord perpendicular to a radius is bisected by it. Let radius $OQ = r$. $NS + OS = ON$. If $NS = 20, 20 + OS = r$, and $OS = 20 - r$. Since OQ is a radius, OQ equals r. $OS^2 + QS^2 = OQ^2, (r-20)^2 + 40^2 = r^2, r^2 - 40r + 400 + 1,600 = r^2$, $2000 = 40r$, and $50 = r$.

37. **D.** Since, the chord is half the diameter, half the chord is half the radius. Draw a right triangle formed by a perpendicular bisector of the chord and the diameter. $x^2+(\frac{1}{2}r)^2 = r^2$, $x^2+\frac{1}{4}r^2 = r^2$, $x^2 = \frac{3}{4}r^2$, $x = \sqrt{\frac{3}{4}r^2}$, and $x = \sqrt{\frac{3}{4}}r = \frac{\sqrt{3}}{2}r$.

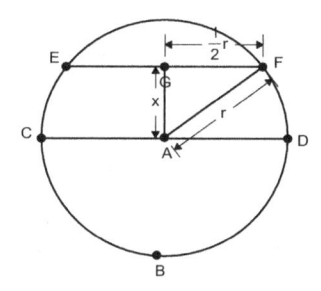

38. **8.** Since MQ is tangent to the radius, angle M is a right angle. Since OMQ is a 30-60-90 right triangle and $OM = 4$, $MQ = 4\sqrt{3}$, and $OQ = 8$.

39. **C.** The area of the triangle is $\frac{1}{2}(4)(4\sqrt{3}) = 8\sqrt{3}$. The area of the circle is $4^2(\pi) = 16\pi$. The area of the sector is $\frac{60}{360} = \frac{x}{16\pi}$, $960\pi = 360x$, and $\frac{8}{3}\pi = x$. The difference between the areas is $8\sqrt{3} - \frac{8}{3}\pi$.

40. **100.** Angles B and C each equal 90 degrees. Since the sum of the angles in a quadrilateral equal 360 degrees, $90 + 90 + 80 + x = 360$, and x is 100 degrees.

41. **5.** To find the length of the arc, $\frac{100}{360} = \frac{x}{18}$, $1800 = 360x$, and $5 = x$.

42. **D.** Since the center is (0,2), subtract 2 from y. To find the radius, $\sqrt{(0-\frac{4}{3})^2 + (2-3)^2} = \sqrt{\frac{16}{9}+1} = \sqrt{\frac{16}{9}+\frac{9}{9}} = \sqrt{\frac{25}{9}} = \frac{5}{3}$. The radius is $\frac{5}{3}$, so the radius squared is $\frac{25}{9}$.

43. **A.** The x-coordinate of the center of the circle is $\frac{1+3}{2} = 2$ and the y-coordinate of the center is $\frac{6+12}{2} = 9$. The center is (2,9). To find the radius, plug in a coordinate such as (1,6). $\sqrt{(2-1)^2 + (9-6)^2} = \sqrt{1+9} = \sqrt{10}$. Radius squared= 10.

161

44. **B.** The radius of the cones and cylinder are 4. The volume of the cylinder is $\pi r^2 h = \pi(4^2)(10) = 160\pi$. The volume of the two cones is $2 \times \frac{1}{3}\pi r^2 h = 2 \times \frac{1}{3}\pi(4)^2(6) = 64\pi$. $160\pi + 64\pi = 224\pi \approx 704$.

45. **420.** If height= h, length = $h + 4$, and width= $h - 7$. The area of the base= lw, so $A = (h + 4)(h - 7) = 42$, $h^2 - 3h - 28 = 42$, $h^2 - 3w - 70 = 0$, and $(h - 10)(h + 7) = 0$. If $h - 10 = 0, h = 10$ and if $h + 7 = 0, h = -7$. Since height can't be negative, height= 10. Length= $h + 4 = 14$ and width= $h - 7 = 3$. Volume= $(10)(14)(3) = 420$.

46. $\frac{3}{5}$. Draw an altitude at B to create two right triangles. Since the base is bisected, each base equals 16 and the hypotenuse is 20. Let the height = x. $16^2 + x^2 = 20^2$, $x^2 = 144$, and $x = 12$. $\sin A = \frac{opposite}{hypotenuse} = \frac{12}{20} = \frac{3}{5}$.

47. **D.** Sin T corresponds to Sin Q which equals $\frac{SR}{SQ}$. To find SQ, $48^2 + 20^2 = SQ^2$, $2{,}704 = SQ^2$, and $52 = SQ$. Thus, $Sin\ Q = \frac{48}{52} = \frac{12}{13}$.

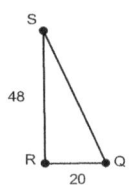

48. **30.** $6a + 12 + 2a + 14 = 90, 8a + 26 = 90, 8a = 64$, and $a = 8$. The smaller angle is $2(8) + 14 = 30$.

49. **C.** $\frac{\pi}{4} \times \frac{180}{\pi} = 45$ degrees. 45 is complementary to 45 since $45 + 45 = 90$.

50. **C.** When an angle is subtracted from a multiple of 2π, such as 6π, it is reflected in the x-axis and sine is negated.

About the Author

Douglas Kovel earned a 99th percentile score on the SAT as a high school senior and was valedictorian of his high school class. He graduated summa cum laude and Phi Beta Kappa from Georgetown University, where he majored in government. He has since completed a graduate certificate in college counseling through the University of San Diego Extension Program. He has taught SAT classes and tutored both independently and for reputable test preparation companies, where he has helped students improve their scores by hundreds of points.

Appendix

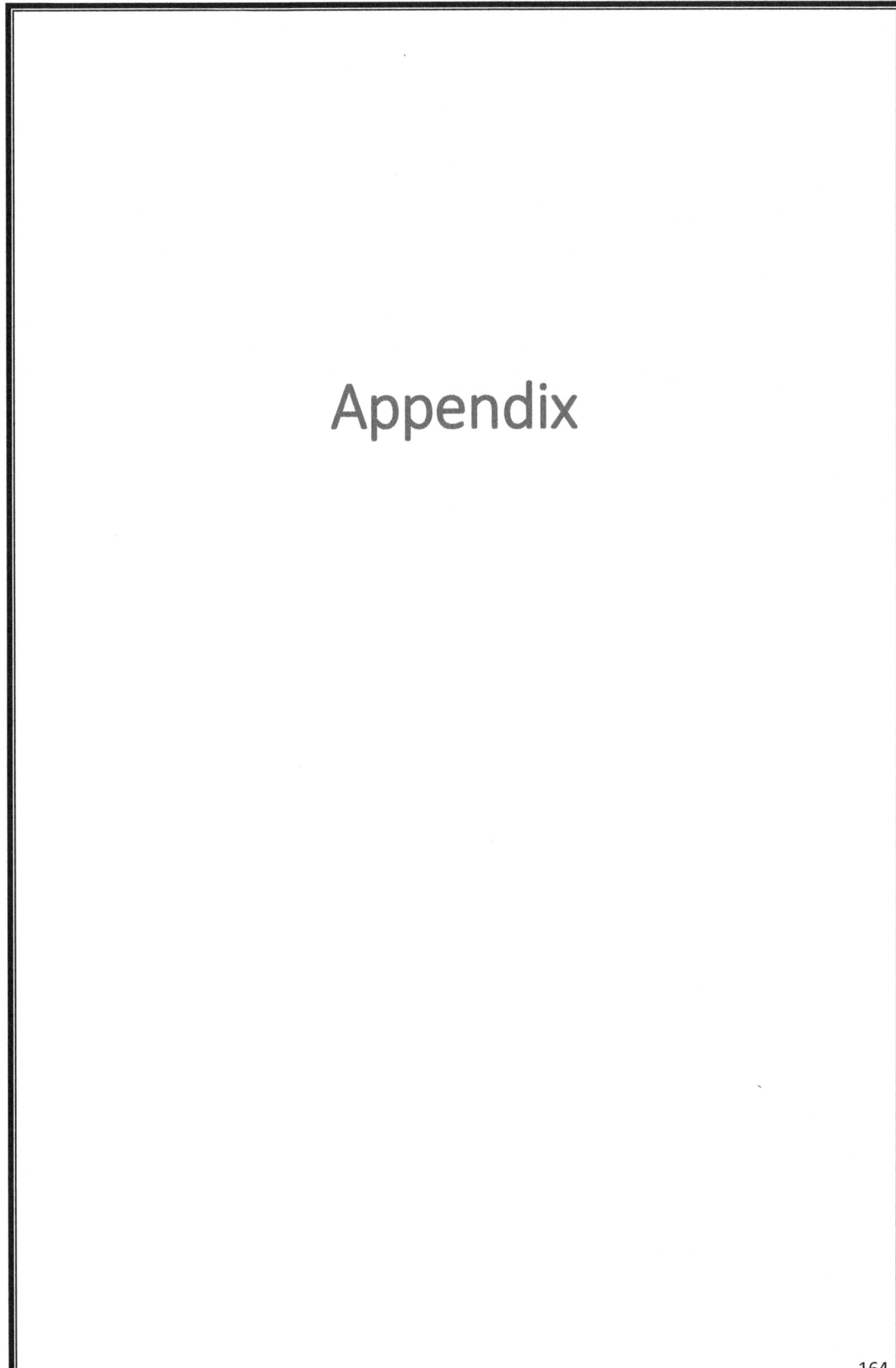

WELCOME TO KWELLER PREP!

Kweller offers Advanced Test Preparation in Small Group Settings

Kweller Prep is a 15-year established supplemental education program with a time-tested record of success. Our results speak for themselves: In 2017, 101 students from the 120 rising eighth graders who enrolled into Kweller Prep received an admission offer to a specialized or top NYC high school program. 33 students from the rising 120 sixth graders who enrolled in Kweller Prep's Hunter High School prep program received an admission offer, making our number of acceptances nearly double that of any competitor. Kweller Prep students in grades 9-12 consistently place into top tier colleges and receive outstanding scholarship offers. We are one of the few test prep centers capable of raising test scores by several hundred points. Each summer, Kweller Prep runs academic full-time camps and hosts weekly parent information sessions and guided college tours. We teach strategies and build a core foundation to make students into better test takers. The Kweller Prep program is designed to help ambitious students excel.

Kweller Prep offers high quality - not high quantity - programs. Tutoring centers, located in Queens in Manhattan, serve as learning incubators where parents, serious students, teachers, tutors, and counselors can learn from one another and grow. Nearly every student at Kweller Prep is the first one in his or her family to attend a specialized high school or top college on scholarship.

Kweller Prep was created in the vision of Frances Kweller, an attorney at law. She was the first one in her immediate family to attend a top college, New York University – Steinhardt School of Education, and to become a lawyer, obtaining her Juris Doctorate from Hofstra University School of Law.

Register for Classes Online:
www.KwellerPrep.com
1(800) 631-1757

About the New SAT

	Evidence-Based Reading and Writing	Math	Essay
Sections	• 65-minute Reading section • 35-minute Writing and Language section	• 25-minute No Calculator section • 55-minute Calculator section	• 50-minute optional essay
Questions	• 52 Questions (Reading) • 44 Questions (Writing and Language)	• 20 Questions (No Calculator) • 38 Questions (Calculator)	• 1 Essay Prompt
Score Range	200-800	200-800	6-24

About the ACT

Section	# of Questions & Time Limit	Content/Skills Covered	Question Types
English	75 questions in 45 min.	Grammar & Usage, Punctuation, Sentence structure, Strategy, Organization, and Style	Four-choice, multiple-choice usage/mechanics and rhetorical skills questions
Math	60 questions in 60 min.	Pre-algebra, elementary algebra, intermediate algebra, coordinate geometry, plane geometry, and trigonometry	Five-choice, multiple-choice questions
Reading	40 questions in 35 min.	Reading comprehension of what is directly stated or implied	Four-choice, multiple-choice referring and reasoning questions
Science	40 questions in 35 min.	Interpretation, analysis, evaluation, reasoning, and problem solving	Our-choice, multiple-choice data representation, research summaries, and conflicting viewpoints questions
Writing (optional)	1 essay in 40 min.	Writing skills	Essay prompt

NEW PSAT-NMSQT

- Who: 11th graders
- Where: At school
- When: Around Oct. 19, Oct. 22, or Nov. 2
- Scholarships: Used by scholarship programs, including the National Merit Scholarship Program, to look for eligible students.

The New PSAT will be a longer test than the old one: It is now 2 hours and 45 minutes. There will be Evidence-Based Reading and Writing in the Reading Test, followed by a Writing and Language Test. There will also be heavy math testing. Bye-bye calculator! The Math Test is now divided into two portions: Math Test – Calculator and Math Test – No Calculator. Do well on this test and you'll qualify for some amazing college scholarships! The New PSAT will have a greater emphasis on the meaning of words in extended contexts and on how word choice shapes meaning, tone, and impact. **There will be no guessing penalty**. The new PSAT will have a rights-only scoring (a point for a correct answer but no deduction for an incorrect answer; blank responses have no impact on scores). The scale ranges for the PSAT/NMSQT and PSAT 10 scores are 320–1520 for the total score, 160–760 for each of two section scores, and 8–38 for test scores.

Kweller suggests: If your school does not offer the PSAT, you can take it at a nearby school for $15. Please contact me if you need help with this.

College Application Help:

Kweller Prep is an expert in the college application process. Unlike many other programs which charge by the hour, we charge a flat rate of $2,500 for up to five colleges ($500 per college), from start to finish, so long as you start your application essays with us by August 1st. This fee includes the editing and re-editing of all personal statements and supplements. It also includes college interview coaching and overall handholding (i.e. "White Glove Service") from start to finish. Interested students must reserve, pay for, and start this service with us by August 1, 2018 so that we can start early. Otherwise, we cannot offer this service and instead can work at an hourly fee at $150 per hour. Our goal in this service is to apply early action, early decision, and early in general. We want our students to be among the first ones submitting college and scholarship applications.

College Application Timeline:

June – August after Junior Year: Select 5 colleges, draft essays and supplements, practice college interview tips, visit colleges, and request letters of recommendation from two to four 10th and 11th grade teachers. Do NOT use teachers from 9th or 12th grade as recommenders. Avoid teachers who hesitate when you ask them to write the letter.

August 1 of Senior Year: Common Application Opens- fill out the college application via www.commonapp.org.

DEADLINE: November 1 of Senior Year: Submit all early action, restrictive early action, and rolling admission college applications.

DEADLINE: December 1 of Senior Year: Macaulay Honors and merit scholarship competitions deadlines

DEADLINE: January 1 of Senior Year: Submit all Regular Decision college applications.

Made in the USA
Middletown, DE
29 May 2019